ABSENT MOTHERS

Funded by the Government of Canada
Financé par la gouvernement du Canada

Demeter Press
140 Holland Street West
P. O. Box 13022
Bradford, ON L3Z 2Y5
Tel: (905) 775-9089
Email: info@demeterpress.org
Website: www.demeterpress.org

Demeter Press logo based on the sculpture "Demeter" by Maria-Luise Bodirsky, www.keramik-atelier.bodirsky.de

Printed and Bound in Canada

Cover photograph: Yarik Mishin
Cover design: Corinna Chong

Library and Archives Canada Cataloguing in Publication

        Absent mothers / Frances Greenslade, editor.

Includes bibliographical references.
ISBN 978-1-77258-123-2 (softcover)

        1. Absentee mothers. I. Greenslade, Frances, 1961-, editor

HQ759.3.A27 2017   306.874'3   C2017-905202-0

MIX
Paper from
responsible sources
FSC
www.fsc.org   FSC® C004071

ABSENT MOTHERS

EDITED BY
Frances Greenslade

DEMETER PRESS, BRADFORD, ONTARIO

Table of Contents

Introduction

FRANCES GREENSLADE

T HE IDEA FOR THIS ANTHOLOGY arose out of a question I have been mulling over for a few years now, specifically since about 2011 when I wrote a novel, *Shelter*, featuring two sisters who are searching for their lost mother. When the book came out and critics began to comment on it, I realized that my book joined the many others that feature absent mothers. Although I understood that my motivation for creating a motherless protagonist stemmed from a desire to make sense of my own mother's death, I wondered why motherless children are so common in literature and film. Do writers simply dispense with mothers as a plot convenience, or is there something deeper going on?

I cast a wide net in my attempt to understand why absent mothers haunt the stories we tell ourselves. The result is a multidisciplinary anthology of voices from several genres—including scholarly essays, personal essays, poetry, and fiction—which explores the perspectives of both motherless children and mothers who have lost their children. Although I didn't expect a definitive answer to my question, as a writer, I believe, as Brigitte Bönisch-Brednich writes in "What to Do with Stories?," that personal stories act "…as a liberation from metanarratives, a chance to empower voices that were not heard, not listened to, before. The deliberate emphasis on stories rather than 'Truths' was and still is a political one, fracturing metanarratives and offering competing and co-existing accounts of experiences" (199). Stories, naturally, are a reflection of our preoccupations, not just as individuals but as collectives. Neal McLeod in *Cree Narrative Memory* explains

1

that "as we find ourselves enmeshed in the trajectories of various stories, we also make contributions to the larger narrative" (11). Thus, the scholarly essays in this collection provide analysis that helps to put the personal stories into a larger context.

Marina Warner argues that absent mothers are predominant in fairy tales because they originate in a time "when death in childbirth was the most common cause of female mortality" (25). That is no longer the case, yet popular literature still favours the motherless child protagonist. The *Harry Potter* series, Claire Cameron's 2014 novel *The Bear*, and *A Series of Unfortunate Events* are some fairly recent examples. Reaching a bit further back, there are the dead mothers of *Anne of Green Gables,* the *Nancy Drew* mysteries, *To Kill a Mockingbird, The Adventures of Tom Sawyer, Great Expectations,* and Kipling's *Kim*, to name only a few, as well as the conveniently absent mothers of *Lord of the Flies, The Lion, the Witch and the Wardrobe,* and *Peter Pan.*

When I recently started reading the *Flavia de Luce* mystery series by Canadian writer Alan Bradley, I was not surprised to find that the intelligent and curious protagonist, Flavia, is also motherless. Her mother died some years earlier in a mountaineering accident. As a reader and as a writer, I understand that Flavia as a character has freer rein as a motherless child; no one is watching her too closely, so she cooks up chemical reactions in the unused wing of her house and experiments with poisons, using her sisters as guinea pigs. Her mother's absence is both an intriguing aspect of character development (essentially unloved, she must fend for herself) and a convenient plot device (no mother to prevent her from riding her beloved bicycle across the countryside at all hours). However, her mother's absence also creates a sense of loneliness and unease for Flavia, a dark thread that runs through the series.

As Berit Åström suggests in her contribution to this antholo-gy, "Dying to Create a Hero: Changing Meanings of Death in Childbirth?," sometimes writers get mothers out of the way early so that the protagonist can get on with her heroic feats. Åström explains that as early as the first century CE, absent mothers were seen as ensuring a heroic path for a child: "According to Pliny the Elder, the greatest gift a mother can bestow on her child is to die in childbirth, preferably painfully." Although we may be tempted to dismiss Pliny's outrageous observation as reflecting ancient ideas, Åström demonstrates the way in which our fiction still sees the mother as an impediment to heroic undertakings. However, I suspect that most fiction writers do not consciously kill their mothers. Rather, the power of that separation continues to resonate into our adult lives so that it shapes the stories and symbols that become our art. In fact, as Esther Ramsay-Jones documents in her essay about older people in dementia care, powerful recollections of mothers and mothering continue to haunt us into our old age.

Recently, I watched Canadian director Patricia Rozema's 2015 film *Into the Forest,* an adaptation from Jean Hegland's near-future, realistic apocalypse novel. The two sisters' mother has, in the recent past, died of an illness, and (spoiler alert) their father is dispatched soon into the film, too. With the power grid shut down and little fuel for their vehicle, the girls are left alone in the deep forest to fend for themselves. Dark, symbolically resonant, but with the forest acting as more of a haven than a threat—at one point the girls retreat into the gnarled hollow of a tree trunk while rain slashes down outside—the film is reminiscent of fairy tales like Hansel and Gretel, Cinderella, and Snow White, which also feature absent mothers. Although the girls' absent mother contributes tension to the plot, the artistic choice to make the mother absent appears to go beyond plot considerations. She seems also to stand for the deep loss and loneliness echoed in their crumbling home and crumbling world. This loss requires them to strike out into the wild, completely without help or guidance, another common theme of fairy tales.

Although the absent mother may appear in many stories as a plot device or as a symbol of the separation of mother and child, their frequent occurrence reveals the anxiety that both mothers and children harbour over this separation. Several of the contributions in this anthology mourn the real and violent separation of Indigenous mothers and children that has occurred in both Canada and Australia. "May Breath: Poetics against Canada's Ongoing Settler Colonial Violence Toward Indigenous Women and Mothers" by Sarah de Leeuw, is a cross-genre lament for Cynthia Gladue, an Indigenous mother of three children who, in 2011, was found dead in a bathtub at a motel along the Yellowhead Highway. De

Leeuw's contribution is a desperate, almost beyond-words plea to pierce the colonial courtroom narrative of Cynthia Gladue's life, to "un-tell" an all-too-common Canadian story. In his contribution, "My Nehiyaw Mother," Randy Lundy writes of the "wind-swept emptiness" left by the absence of his Cree mother in the 1970s on the Canadian prairies. Lundy explains that he "certainly had no idea what her voice might sound like or what it might feel like to be held by her." He was "raised in complete ignorance of [his] maternal ancestors and [his] Indigenous heritage." In her essay about Jane Harrison's play *Stolen,* Emma Dalton demonstrates the deliberate effort of Australia's stolen generation of Indigenous children to remember their mothers and of their mothers' efforts to remember their children. These pieces reveal the heartbreak of marginalized Indigenous mothers and children in Canada and Australia. They highlight the reality of mothers who are absent because of violent colonial policies and practices. But telling the stories, as the writers do in this collection, is also one way to begin to expose "the poison" of colonialism, which, in the epigraph to his 1989 play *Dry Lips Oughta Move To Kapuskasing,* playwright Tomson Highway suggests is necessary for healing (6). The telling, as Dalton explains in her essay, is a path to remembering the lives and experiences of mothers and children who have been subject to colonial policies of forced forgetting.

Themes of forgetting and remembering also run through "Mother India," written by Subimal Misra and translated by V. Ramaswamy. In one of the stories within the piece, a boy remembers a brutal attack in India on his mother, and vows, "Let me grow up a bit, let me get strong ... Mother's told me, it's I who have to take revenge." His words echo those of Jo-Ann Episkenew in her book *Taking Back our Spirits: Indigenous Literature, Public Policy, and Healing.* Episkenew writes, "Because I was painfully aware of the injuries that colonialism and racism had inflicted on Indigenous communities, I was hell-bent to discover where these arrogant attitudes originated and establish who was to blame" (1). The stories in this anthology do not end with blame, however. They move towards recognizing and, ultimately, repairing the deep wound in the most primal of human relationships. As Episkenew explains:

I began to learn something that I believe is more important and certainly more productive than finding out who is to blame. I began to understand the healing power of stories in general and of Indigenous literature in particular....Not only does Indigenous literature respond to and critique the policies of the government of Canada; it also functions as 'medicine' to help cure the colonial contagion by healing the communities that these policies have injured. (2)

Another type of maternal absence poignantly portrayed in several pieces in this collection stems from the rejection of the mother role. Whether deliberate and obvious or subtle and perhaps even unintentional, the rejection of the mother role engenders confusion and feelings of betrayal that reverberate into our adult lives. Bianca Batti's essay on the maternal corpses in William Faulkner's *As I Lay Dying* and Suzan-Lori Parks's *Getting Mother's Body* examines the uneasy ambivalence that characterizes many women's memories of their own mothers' so-called transgressions. She writes that

even today, the "bad" mother comes to be defined in opposition to the true woman—the "good" mother—in that the bad mother is perceived as not selfless enough, not pure enough, not submissive enough, not domestic enough, not white enough, not middle class enough. The bad mother does not conform to the norms imposed upon women through the Victorian cult of "true womanhood"—norms that persist to this day.

In Bernadette Wagner's "Blue Robe," for example, the narrator accidentally discovers her mother, who has had an affair with her boss, packing her suitcases one afternoon to leave home before her children get out from school. The narrator's continued ambivalence, her adult search for understanding her mother's motives, is implicit in the vivid remembered details and in her memory of her mother's words: "I know you're going to hate me for this!" Courtney Bates-Hardy's poem "Mother-Witch," as well as her other poems, provides a kind of counterpoint to Wagner's piece. A reflection on both mothering and writing, "Mother-Witch" begins: "Sometimes I hate them: my children and their chirping open mouths." Ironically, through their use of the simple word "hate," both authors hint at much muddier emotions, which suggests that the struggle to make sense of emotions not congruent with the socially acceptable norms of the "good mother."

The emotional turmoil and grief of separated mothers and children is further captured in "Notes from Tinkle," by Madhulika Liddle, and in two memoir pieces by Monica Meneghetti. In "Notes from Tinkle," a mother who has been separated from her son by an impending divorce finds a reflection of her own feelings of grief in a mysterious child, whom she discovers has been separated from her mother by poverty. "Mushrooms and Memory" and "The Orchard" portray the rich memories of a daughter who has been separated from her mother both by illness and the passage of time; Meneghetti's pieces suggest the writer's uncertainty about her childhood role in her relationship with her mother, and her longing to understand it.

The voices in this anthology form a hybrid of the close-up, grounded details of the lived stories of absent mothers and motherless children, and the reflective, scholarly perspective that helps to put our stories into a larger context. The stories we tell ourselves can trap us, or they can free us. So can the stories that others tell about us. The potent pieces gathered here witness, remember, mourn, and critique, and in so doing, they reshape the dominant narrative about absent mothers.

WORKS CITED

Bönisch-Brednich, Brigitte. "What to Do with Stories?" *Fabula*, vol. 57, no. 3-4, 2006, pp. 195-215.

Episkenew, Jo-Ann. *Taking Back our Spirits: Indigenous Literature, Public Policy, and Healing.* University of Manitoba Press, 2009.

Highway, Tomson. *Dry Lips Oughta Move To Kapuskasing*. Fifth House, 1989.

Warner, Marina. "The Absent Mother: Women against Women in Old Wives' Tales." *History Today. History Today*, vol. 41, no. 4, 1991, pp. 22-28.

Dying to Create a Hero

Changing Meanings of Death in Childbirth?

BERIT ÅSTRÖM

A CCORDING TO PLINY THE ELDER, the greatest gift a mother can bestow on her child is to die in childbirth, preferably painfully. In his first-century CE book *History of Nature*, he rates such a death as highly auspicious, promising a great future for the child, citing Julius Caesar and Scipio Africanus as examples of how the mother's destruction ensures the son's success (192). This idea of the hero who loses his mother at birth has been recirculated through centuries of Western literary history, including, for example, the Arthurian knight of sorrows, Tristram, and Macduff, the man who defeats Macbeth. In his latest incarnation on film (2011), Conan the Barbarian also loses his mother at the moment of his birth. In this chapter, I read Conan against earlier traditions of motherless heroes, and discuss the implications of the film makers' choice to kill a mother whom her creator, Robert E. Howard, left alive and well. I also contrast the 2011 version of the dying mother to literary dead mothers of earlier centuries.

The 2011 mother is a warrior, not a cipher or just a vessel for her husband's seed to be discarded after delivering the son. Her death is framed as a sacrifice that confers increased hero status on her son. Yet what appears to be a reinterpretation, a valorization of the dying mother, does not alter the fact that, like so many other heroes in recent years, Conan is left to be raised by a father; their relationship becomes focus of the film. Rather than reflecting an upgrade of the mother's status, Conan's dead mother seems to be just another victim of what Hannah Hamad has termed "postfeminist fatherhood" —a valorization of fathers that is predicated on the marginalization of mothers (1).

DEAD MOTHERS IN CULTURAL AND LITERARY HISTORY

Throughout Western history, patriarchal society has regarded mothers as problematic. As scholars, such as Katherine Park, have shown, the medical profession, as well as laypeople, has worried not only about the mother's sexual fidelity but also about her body's effects on the unborn fetus. As a result, much effort has been spent regulating the mother's behaviour in order to protect the child's physical and mental health (Åström, "Corrupte Mylke"). But the mother remains problematic even after the birth of the child. The belief that mothers cannot raise boys to men is prevalent throughout history, and remains to this day (Kimmel 150). It is not surprising, therefore, that the boy who grows up without a mother is seen to have a great future, or as Janet Adelman phrases it, "heroic masculinity turns on leaving the mother behind" (130). A prerequisite for achieving hero status is to reject the mother, emotionally and physically.

Thomas Mallory expresses this idea of rejecting the maternal in his 1471 version of the King Arthur story. The pregnant Queen Elizabeth sets out to find her husband Meliodas, who has been kidnapped. While travelling in the wilderness, she goes into labour and gives birth to a son whom she names Tristram. Realizing she is about to die, she says to the boy "thou hast murdered thy mother, and therefore thou that art a murderer so young, thou art likely to be a manly man in thine age" (304). The infant has proven himself to be able to kill at a young age, which shows promise for his adulthood: he will be not only a man but a manly man. And most important of all, he has murdered his mother. He has rejected her and, in so doing, has protected himself from her potentially harmful influence.

Another example of a hero who leaves his mother behind is William Shakespeare's Macduff, who is the only man powerful enough to kill the tyrant Macbeth. This power derives from his status as a man not born of a woman. As the witches have told Macbeth, only a man not of woman born may kill him, and

Macduff claims to be such a man.[1] The power inherent in such a birth is related to a patriarchal fantasy of "an all-male family, composed of nothing but males," as Janet Adelman notes in her analysis of *Macbeth* (139). In this fantasy, men would ideally not have to rely on women to reproduce. This idea of men being the sole progenitors of children is of long standing. An early written record is Aeschylus's fifth-century BCE play *The Eumenides*. In it, Apollo proclaims that only the father is the true parent of the child. The mother is only the vessel, the nurse of the seed that the father has sown. In his attempt to excuse Orestes's murder of his mother, Apollo makes it clear that mother and child are no more related than strangers. In the fourth century BCE, Aristotle adds scientific weight to Apollo's claims, stating that "reasoning and observed fact" show that the father is the one who "generates" the child through his semen, whilst the mother is the one "out of which it generates" (*Generation*, 113, 111). Although the mother may contribute the space for the fetus to grow in, and the soil, so to speak, in which it grows, it is the father who is the child's creator, just as the carpenter creates a bedstead out of wood (113). These texts display a desire to eradicate the mother's involvement in human reproduction. On a more everyday level, this is, of course, not possible. A way of minimizing the maternal impact, however, is to remove the child from the mother's body at the first available moment. Such is the birth of Macduff. Although he obviously grew inside a woman's body, he was at least "untimely ripped" from his mother's womb (5.10.16). As Adelman notes, in an echo of Pliny: "violent separation from the mother is the mark of the successful male" (144). It is thus not enough to be born early; the birth must also be violent. A man who can carve, or rip, his way out of his mother, such as Macduff does, or kill his mother, as Tristram does, has secured a heroic future for himself.

Being born this way also ensures that the mother dies. Until very recently, women did not survive a Caesarean section. In some literary cases, they are already dead when they give birth, as is for example Coronis, the mother of Asclepius, the god of medicine. Apollo, the father of the unborn Asclepius, kills Coronis when he finds out that she has been unfaithful. As she lies on the funeral pyre, he decides to save the boy by cutting him out from her corpse

(Edelstein and Edelstein 4, 31). Thus, in these various stories, sons are rescued from the potentially harmful influence of their mothers. Being "prematurely deprived of a nurturing maternal presence" is what gives a man power (Adelman 144); it saves him from the potentially feminizing effects of the mother.

CONAN AND THE TRADITION OF DEAD MOTHERS

Unlike the heroes mentioned so far, the original Conan appears to have had a mother who survived giving birth to him. The character was created by prolific pulp fiction author Robert E. Howard. Between 1932 and 1935, Howard wrote twenty-one stories about the character; they were set in a prehistoric period called the Hyborian age. Most of the stories were published in the pulp magazine *Weird Tales*. It appears that Howard himself was not really interested in Conan's immediate family background, stating that the character "seemed to step full-grown into my consciousness" (qtd. in Jones 907).[2] Howard's Conan is an adult who does not need parents, and the only reference to his mother is oblique. In the story "Black Colossus," Conan says that he "was born in the midst of a battle" and that the "first sound my ears heard was the clang of swords and the yells of the slaying" (Howard 116). No further information is given as to the fate of his mother, as Howard has simply stated that Conan "was born on a battle field, during a fight between his tribe and a horde of raiding Vanir" (Jones 900). Later developments of the character— including fan-created timelines constructing an internal chronology for the stories, which Howard set in no particular order—continue this tradition (Bertetti 23). This fan work is also the basis for the later Dark Horse *Conan* comic books (24). In these comics, published from 2003 onward, the mother has been given a name, Fialla, and is introduced as fighting alongside her husband in a border skirmish. When she goes into labour, the men in her tribe protect her, and the circumstances of his birth are taken as an omen that the boy will become a great warrior ("Fialla"). At the time of writing, she is still alive.

Regardless of Howard's own narrative preferences regarding mothers, he places Conan "within a Western prototypical heroic pattern" (Elliott 52). Thus, when the Conan stories were adapted into the film *Conan the Barbarian* in 1982, the conventions of Western narrative tradition came into play. These conventions demand that heroes grow up without mothers (Åström, "Symbolic Annihilation"), so the young Conan is forced to watch his mother be decapitated by the main villain, Thulsa Doom. The 2011 version retains the dead mother, and kills her even earlier, during the prologue and before the opening credits. Yet unlike, for example, Queen Elizabeth, Macduff's mother, or Coronis, the 2011 Fialla is not weak, unnamed, or adulterous. She is a warrior, clad in leather and metal armour, fighting in the battle alongside her husband, Corin, and other members of their barbarian tribe. When her assailant stabs her in the belly, she retaliates and kills him with her own sword. When Corin comes to her aid, she tells him, "I want to see my child before I die." She then hands him her knife so that he can open up her belly and free the child. She holds the baby and names him, before dying. In contrast to the other mothers mentioned, she is an active subject who makes demands and chooses the place and manner of her death. The unnamed mother in the 1982 version of *Conan* appears transfixed by Thulsa Doom's gaze and meekly allows herself to be decapitated. The 2011 Fialla, however, kills her own murderer. Despite her brief presence on the screen, Fialla's words and actions make her a memorable character and present her as a hero.

This heroism is evoked later in the film. Conan's friend Artus uses the way Fialla died to explain Conan's extraordinary bravery and fighting skills to the heroine, Tamara: "Most men are born to their mother's milk. His first taste was of his mother's blood. He was battleborn."[3] Because Conan was born during a battle and because she gave her life for him, he is a hero. This is not an attempt by Artus to make Tamara feel sorry for Conan for having lost his mother, nor is it perceived that way by her. Her response is that a birth in battle renders Conan unfit for anything but killing. Although the two characters view warfare and killing differently, both Artus and Tamara regard the mother's heroic action as conferring hero status onto her son.

Up to this point, it is tempting to read this reinterpretation of the death in childbirth trope as a valorization of the mother. Yet there are complications. As has already been noted, a mother's nurture may make a man weak. One form that this dangerous nurture may take is breastfeeding. Western societies have long distrusted breastmilk, often viewing it as poisonous for the infant. Although the mother's milk is ideally the best nourishment for the infant, medical texts, as well as lay traditions from the Middle Ages onward, have expressed fear that breastmilk could cause illness or death. The milk was also suspected of making sons effeminate (Åström, "Corrupte Mylke"). These fears have continued into the present time, and are particularly prevalent in newspapers and online forums for pregnant and new mothers.[4] Viewed in this light, Artus's comment that Conan did not taste his mother's milk, only her blood, takes on a more sinister tone. Since Conan did not nurse at his mother's breast, he has not imbibed a substance that may make him effeminate or ill. He has grown up strong and masculine.

Conan's birth also features Adelman's "violent separation" of son from mother. The film's opening sequence, detailing the ancient history leading up to the film's events, segues into an image of a child floating in a womb. This womb is pierced by a sword. The next shot is of Fialla's attacker pulling the sword out of her belly. Just like Macduff, Conan is untimely ripped from his mother. Thus, even though she chooses to have the child cut from her, rather than let it die with her, the son is separated from her through violence to live on with his father, whereas she dies.

That Howard's Conan is transformed into a hero who loses his mother early, a mother from whom he is separated violently, may be seen as a reflection of what film scholar Hannah Hamad has termed "postfeminist fatherhood." Hamad argues that beginning in the early years of the twenty-first century, a new type of hero, the postfeminist father, has begun to appear in films. This is a character whose masculinity is based on his ability to nurture and care for his children: he is "emotionally articulate, domestically competent, skilled in managing the quotidian practicalities of parenthood" (2). Although Corin is never shown to change nappies, he has successfully raised his son as only a man can. He has taught him to fight with swords, and more importantly, he is not afraid to tell his son that he loves him. It appears that after the mother's death, father and son have lived together without the need of any maternal figure. This lack of mothers, and the privileging of fathers, is a prominent feature of postfeminist fatherhood narratives, Hamad notes (3). In order for fathers to reach their full potential, mothers must be marginalized or removed completely.

Western heroic narratives, thus, require that sons leave their mothers behind, embrace their fathers' heritage and avenge their deaths. This is what happens to Conan in both the 1982 and the 2011 filmic versions of the story. As Nicky Falkoff notes, although the 1982 Conan is somewhat unfocused in his endeavours, his quest is to avenge his father, and when he faces Thulsa Doom, his parents' murderer, he charges him with the deaths of his father and his tribe but he does not mention his mother (128, 132). In the 2011 version, Fialla has avenged herself against her killer, an insignificant raider, so there is no need for Conan to seek revenge for her death. The narrative instead constructs a drawn-out death scene in which Corin sacrifices himself for his son, when the villain Khalar Zym steals his sword and the ancient artefact he has been guarding. Corin's death subsequently haunts Conan for many years, until he manages to track down Khalar Zym, take back the sword and kill him. With this task completed, Conan chooses not to settle down with Tamara, who evidently wishes him to do so, but to return to his father's tomb to show that the sword has been retrieved. What happens afterward is anybody's guess, but the narrative appears to suggest that communing with one's father's spirit is more important than forming relationships with the living. A dead father, thus, trumps a living girlfriend, whereas a dead mother is soon forgotten.

At first glance, Fialla's character, manner of death, and the way she is evoked later, all suggest that the trope of the propitious maternal death in childbirth is being subverted. However, this subversion is at best superficial. Fialla is as marginal as Queen Elizabeth, Macduff's mother, and Coronis. And the character who has any lasting effect on Conan is his father. He is the parent who teaches him about sword fighting and everything else he needs to know. Corin is the parent whose expectations and standards Conan wishes to live up to. It is true that in the Hyborian world that Howard created, there are "no mothers, grandmothers, aunts ...

and only a couple of sisters of any merit" (Elliott 58), but at least in Howard's universe, the adult Conan rejects all family members equally. He has no need of either father or mother. It is the film makers of the late twentieth and early twenty-first century who make the character fall in line with all the other heroes who must reject their mothers and embrace their fathers. It appears that Pliny's claim still holds true: it is an excellent omen for a child if his mother dies violently and painfully. At least on film.

ENDNOTES

[1]It is usually assumed that he was born through a Caesarean section.
[2]Frank Coffman, however, has shown how Conan grew out of Howard's early writing.
[3]Fans of Robert E. Howard state emphatically that the fact that the 2011 Conan was birthed through a Caesarean section rather than vaginally means that he is not battle born, which would be a break with the whole mythos (Harron).
[4]See for example Williams on pesticides, Patience on HIV, and Gladstone on maternal stress hormones, and their potential effects on breastfed children.

WORKS CITED

Aeschylus. *The Eumenides*. Translated by G. Theodoridis. *Poetry in Translation*, 2017, www.poetryintranslation.com/PITBR/Greek/Eumenides.htm. Accessed 28 June 2017.

Aristotle. *Generation of Animals*. Translated by A. I. Peck. William Heinemann Ltd, 1902, *Archive*, archive.org/details/generationofanim00arisuoft. Accessed 28 June 2017.

Åström, Berit. "'Sucking the Corrupte Mylke of an Infected Nurse': Regulating the Maternal Body in Western Culture." *Journal of Gender Studies*, vol. 24, no. 5, 2015, pp. 574-86.

Åström, Berit "The Symbolic Annihilation of Mothers in Popular Culture: *Single Father* and the Death of the Mother." *Feminist Media Studies*, vol. 15, no. 4, 2015, pp. 593-607.

Adelman, Janet. *Suffocating Mothers: Fantasies of Maternal Origin in Shakespeare's Plays*, Hamlet *to* The Tempest. Routledge, 1992.

Bertetti, Paolo. "*Conan the Barbarian*: Transmedia Adventures of a Pulp Hero." *Transmedia Archaeology: Storytelling in the Borderlines of Science Fiction, Comics and Pulp Magazines*, edited by Carlos Scolari et al., Palgrave Macmillan, 2014, pp. 15-38.

Coffman, Frank. "Barbarism Ascendant: The Poetic and Epistolary Origins of the Character and His World." *Conan Meets the Academy: Multidisciplinary Essays on the Enduring Barbarian*, edited by Jonas Prida, McFarland, 2013, pp. 35-50.

Conan the Barbarian. Directed by John Milius, Universal Pictures, 1982.

Conan the Barbarian. Directed by Marcus Nispel, NU Image/ Millennium Films, 2011.

Edelstein, Emma J., and Ludwig Edelstein. *Asclepius: Collection and Interpretation of the Testimonies*. The Johns Hopkins University Press, 1998.

Elliott, Winter. "Life, Liberty, and the Pursuit of Women: Gender Dynamics in the Hyborian World." *Conan Meets the Academy: Multidisciplinary Essays on the Enduring Barbarian*, edited by Jonas Prida, McFarland, 2013, pp. 51-9.

Falkoff, Nicky. "Arnold at the Gates: Subverting Star Persona in *Conan the Barbarian*." *Conan the Barbarian: Multidisciplinary Essays on the Enduring Barbarian*, edited by Jonas Prida, MacFarland, 2013, pp. 125-43.

"Fialla." *Comicvine*, 2017, www.comicvine.com/fialla/4005-53213. Accessed 28 June 2017.

Gladstone, Sarah. "Bad Breasts?! New Study Finds Breastmilk is Passing Stress to Newborns." *Ravishly*,15 Feb. 2014, www. ravishly.com/2015/09/07/bad-breasts-new-study-finds-breast-milk-passing-stress-newborns. Accessed 28 June 2017.

Hamad, Hannah. *Postfeminism and Paternity in Contemporary U.S. Film: Framing Fatherhood*. Routledge, 2014.

Harron, Al. "It is the End of All Hope." *The Blog That Time Forgot*, 29 Oct. 2009, theblogthattimeforgot.blogspot.se/2009/10/it-is-end-of-all-hope.html. Accessed 28 June 2017.

Howard, Robert E. *The Complete Chronicles of Conan*. Edited by Stephen Jones. Gollanz, 2006.

Jones, Stephen. "Afterword: Robert E. Howard and Conan." *The Complete Chronicles of Conan*, edited by Stephen Jones,

Gollanz, 2006, pp. 897-925.

Kimmel, Michael. *Angry White Men: American Masculinity at the End of an Era.* Nation Books, 2013.

Park, Katherine. *Secrets of Women: Gender, Generation, and the Origins of Human Dissection.* Zone Books, 2006.

Patience, Martin. "When Mom Can't, Or Won't, Breast-Feed, Firm Has Option." *Chicago Tribune*, 11 Apr. 2004, articles. chicagotribune.com/2004-04-11/features/0404110416_1_wet-nurses-breast-milk-bottle-fed-babies. Accessed 11 May 2016.

Pliny the Elder. *Pliny's Natural History in Thirty-Seven Books.* The Wernerian Club, 1847, *Archive*, archive.org/stream/plinysnaturalhis00plinrich#page/n7/mode/2up. Accessed 28 June 2017.

Shakespeare, William. *Macbeth.* Edited by Bernard Lott, Longman, 1965.

Williams, Florence. "Toxic Breastmilk?" *The New York Times*, 9 Jan. 2005, www.nytimes.com/2005/01/09/magazine/09TOXIC. html?_r=1. Accessed 11 May 2016.

"Is Mother All Right?"

An Exploration of the Maternal Figure
—Absent yet Present—in Dementia Care

ESTHER RAMSAY-JONES

*T*HE OLD LADY IS SEATED *at the dining table. She is making a chewing motion with her lips but is eating nothing. She calls out, "Is Mother all right?" Nobody answers. The two carers are in the kitchen taking the temperature of the food. The old lady grabs the fork in front of her, repositions it on the table and then presses her left hand flat down on it; then she moves her right hand and places it on top of the knife. She picks up the knife and encircles the top of her glass with it. "Is Mother all right?" A carer, dishing up, walks past and says, "Yes, your mum's fine."*

In my observations of older people living with dementia, I have frequently noticed residents calling out for a mother who is physically absent, no longer alive. In reality, these mothers are dead, and their own children are soon to die.

Scenes such as these—where there is a muddling, or merger, of past and present lives and distant memories of being mothered, of having had mothers and, for some, of having been a mother to a child—have been a striking reminder to me of who, and how, we are at our most fundamental. We are always babies to mothers, always at some level connected—by the very nature of the in utero experience—to them.

As Bracha Ettinger argues, it is perhaps our earliest, preverbal encounter with the reverberations of the womb, and the life-sustaining force of the umbilical upon which we depend, that leaves an originary psychic trace of interdependency (2-3). This experience involves the co-becoming and co-creating of two subjects linked and unlinked. It forms a trace, in our mind and in our

17

memory, which is arguably impossible to obliterate. A structure of interdependence is at the root of human life. Although there may be maternal or parental failings and, for some, experiences of neglect from birth onward, in our ending days, we may at a deeply unconscious level yearn for a return to a space in which another encounters us and is with us; that, in finitude, one final holding experience (Winnicott 37) allows us to un-become; that there is some felt presence of a motherlike encompassing in the moment of our very absence.

In "The Old Fools," Philip Larkin recognizes that the minds of older people house memories of people from lives gone by:

> Perhaps, being old is having lighted rooms
> Inside your head, and people in them acting
> That is where they live
> Not here and now but when all happened once. (131)

This chapter explores the way in which the maternal figure presents herself to elders in dementia care, despite the reality of her concrete absence. As people with dementia become increasingly dependent, I want to demonstrate that the maternal figure takes on a more powerful presence in the erratically lighted rooms of fragmenting minds. However, care workers sometimes resort to defensive modes of functioning, which are systematically assembled at the level of the organization of the labour process because of the intolerable levels of anxiety brought about by the very nature of the work itself (Menzies Lyth 99). When care workers feel overburdened by the emotional labour of the care work, they may avoid responding to the repetitive calls of the older people who cry out for their mothers. Of course, it is not always the case that care workers distance themselves from these palpable communications of dependency from those in their care. For balance, this chapter will include some encounters that demonstrate what Anne Alvarez may consider a "presence," an aliveness in the care staff (qtd in Maiello 185), which mirrors something of an instinctive knowingness that a mother can demonstrate in response to her baby. I would argue, therefore, that maternal qualities, of many guises, are noticeable in the daily practice of care work. For the purposes of this chapter, all vignettes from the observational study are in italics.

DAPHNE: MOTHERS PRESENT IN ABSENCE

Mothers with different qualities seemed to haunt both the culture and the minds of the residents in the first organization, a London care home, which I observed psychodynamically (Bick; Hinshelwood and Skogstad; Datler et al; Davenhill) in my role as a researcher. Care staff or other residents came to represent the particularity of mothers once known. Internalized, yet absent mothers, were often around. This is not to say that other family members were invalidated or unimportant. Absent fathers and siblings were also located in those living and working in the home. The home often reminded me of a "matrixial field" (Ettinger 2)—a psychic landscape made up of deeply embedded memories from divergent family albums. But the maternal memory was most frequently replayed and represented in daily life.

Over several months, I observed two particular residents, Daphne and Dorothy, both pseudonyms, in two different sites. Daphne was an English woman in her eighties. She was well educated, a former teacher, and had lived in London all her life. She had no children but had had a long partnership with Benjamin, now too frail to look after her. Daphne was charming, well versed in Shakespeare, and wanted to belong. She often tried to help others and joined in activities in the home regularly.

She also recognized, at a partially conscious level, her own need to be helped and regularly spoke of her underlying belief in interdependence. She was unable to put this into words precisely, but she commented on moments of reciprocal care that she had observed. She seemed to relish these moments. I sensed that Daphne benefitted from being in the home. Nonetheless she often became very anxious and tearful, as if abandoned. It was at those times that she tended to call upon her lost mother. She projected onto an internalized mother all of her own anxieties and ill feeling.

When fearful, Daphne found it impossible to articulate her experience in words and was barely recognizable as the resident still able to quote Shakespeare. I sometimes likened her in my mind to a smaller child, struggling to speak. She seemed in need of a mother able to help her reflect on her experience, to digest her raw projections and, in a Bionian sense, to contain them (qtd in Ogden 145). Mothers, then, though missing in practice, were occasionally and helpfully brought to life as mothers able to contain unprocessed emotion.

AN ANXIOUS MOTHER

In the following sequence, Daphne had come back from a morning out with Benjamin. They had had a good time at the cinema. On return, though, Daphne was confused: why was Benjamin no longer with her? She felt lost, at sea. She started to summon up her absent mother. Daphne imagined her mother worrying about her being lost. What follows is directly observed material.

She looks sad. "I am worried that my mother will be worrying about me, not being home," says Daphne. She says nothing more. I move close, standing with her for a few moments. She starts walking out of the main lounge, and I walk by her side.

Of course, Daphne could be replacing Benjamin with her mother, for he too could plausibly be concerned. I would suggest, though, that through the imagined figure of her mother, Daphne can express her own anxious feelings. She can retreat into being a child, expressing her feelings of dependence on another, who can help her to achieve a more comfortable psychic state. Eventually, I sidled up to Daphne, sensing in her a perturbing aloneness. My body's movements say, "I am here with you."

SHIFTING MOTHERS

Another resident in the same care home as Daphne shifted, one day, from being Mother with a son to being a child with a mother. In the next scene, we see that the impending lunch reminded Oona of her loneliness. Oona's identity was intertwined with both her son and her mother; she seemed to be both an absent mother and an absent daughter simultaneously. This gives us, perhaps, some insight into the daily reality of dementia—the gaping sense of absence that comes to mark people's experiences. It was also possible that

Oona symbolized something of the wider organizational culture of the home and a longing for more nurturing therein. Who knows? The carer, in the following vignette, made every effort to reassure Oona about her son, who did visit the home, this reassurance eventually allowed to Oona to settle and to take her seat. In this instance, the carer became a mother able to take note of Oona's anxiety. But the more Oona thought about the lunchtime setting, the more she thought of a mum alone. Herself perhaps.

A carer helps her to get to her seat. Oona stands looking at the table. She says to a carer, "But what about my son?" The carer smiles at Oona, "He will be here after lunch; I'm sure that he is due then. There is no need to worry. He will be coming." Oona is relieved and begins to sit down.

As she sits waiting at the table with one other sleeping resident, she looks at the knives and forks and says, "Oh, but what about Mum, she will be so very lonely all by herself at lunchtime without me."

MOTHERS IN OTHERS

At times, Daphne revived a mother who was relaxed, settling in. The function of Daphne's shadowy mother was to be a mirror to her own experience, which was resonant of the mirroring micro-interactions between a mother and a newborn baby (Winnicott 37). When the quality of relating is going well, Mother is able to re-present to the baby a mirror image of his or her feelings. This process is thought to allow the baby to get to know his or her self through mother's attuned responses. In other words, Mother has understood baby's state of mind. On the other hand, the mirror that Mother holds up can also be one that is distorted. This was not usually the case, however, with Daphne's resurrected mother.

Daphne walks up to Rayna, a short lady possibly from the Indian subcontinent, and stands with her. She says, "Hello." Daphne walks back to where I am sitting in the back of the room. Daphne sits near me. She is watching Rayna, who is walking about and looking as if she is trying to find someone. "My mum," Daphne says about Rayna, looking at her with a gentle expression on her face; her lips turned in to a slight smile, eyes soft. "It's good, I suppose, really, at least Mum gets to know lots of new people now. It can't be bad."

On this occasion, Daphne herself was at ease and seemed to experience the care home in a positive way. Daphne took notice of her environment and the people in it, in much the same way that I spent my time noticing her, taking her in. There was, it seemed, a ripple effect of noticing, which was mirrorlike in itself. Here Rayna becomes Daphne's mother, a mother and child able to separate, both individuated enough to meet new people.

LOST CHILDREN, LOST MOTHERS

The experience of dementia is one in which loss is encountered, both for the people with dementia and, of course, for those who love them. There is the loss of memory, the loss of once-known identities, sometimes the loss of speech and bodily movement, the loss of place in space and contemporary time, and for residents in a care home, the loss of home and of familiar objects. Mothers and fathers, too, who died many years ago, can sometimes be lost over again as the unbearable realization of deaths resurface.

The experience of lost objects and lost people is encapsulated in the following observation. One day Daphne searched for a way to get home. Her lost coat symbolized her own feeling of being lost. And Mother, a representative of home, had not arrived as Daphne waited at the main entrance door to the care home. The phantasized mother that Daphne conjured up seemed to be the only one who would be able to find her. As we will see, I interrupted this phantasy insensitively and it was met with Daphne's anger; her agency intact, she was nonetheless clear about what she does not want.

These kinds of phantasy could have defensive, protective functions (Dartington 151). It possibly allowed Daphne to avoid feeling so utterly helpless. The imagined Mother became a rescuer. I wondered if Daphne knew at a frighteningly profound level that that part of her which was once able to rescue her (a greater independence, let's say) was diminishing, as the condition progressed.

I walk with Daphne around the corridor. She is very anxious that she has lost her coat. For some time before this she was standing at the front door looking out, commenting that she was waiting for her mother to get her back home again.

As we walk around the corridor, a carer tells her that it is lunchtime. Daphne gets upset and storms off, saying, "I am not having my lunch here, no I'm not." She looks at me, and says, "I thought you were my friend."

She comes back to where I am standing. I ask her if she might want to have lunch here today while she waits. (She asks the manager if she can phone her mother).

"No," she says, pushing her arm to the left as if to push away my suggestion, "My mum gets me my lunch every day and she wouldn't know where I'd got to."

OUT OF TOUCH MOTHERS

Daphne often spoke to me poetically. Her observations of the environment were very moving. I had learned that Benjamin, her partner, had died days before the scene which follows. Daphne had been crying in the dining room, and she seemed scared. Staff members were busy, and no one knew what to do with Daphne's (wordless) grief. Care workers were trying, but nothing could stop the flow of tears. The manager had also attempted to cuddle Daphne, but this physical closeness had upset her. Perhaps only Benjamin would do.

In the end, the activities coordinator suggested involving Daphne in a group trip to a local coffee shop. Daphne had agreed to this. She did not want to experience her own isolation. The activities coordinator had brought Daphne into the reception area, near the front door, where she stood with other residents also about to go out. Daphne was left here as staff went to collect residents' coats. Daphne, I thought, felt abandoned and alone again as she waited in the reception space.

"Their worlds don't understand my world; my world doesn't understand theirs," says Daphne. "They are too busy. They can't pay attention to you." She begins to make this quivering, anxious noise again. She is holding her hands together tightly around her. She begins to look at an empty chair, while the carer is getting one of the ladies ready. "I can't see Mum," she says.

It was impossible for the carers to attend to Daphne in the way she needed.

The care workers were busy, carrying out the physical tasks involved in a trip out on a cold day. The emotional and psychic turmoil that Daphne was experiencing had a small place there in the home, in that moment. She needed a mother present to her "world," one that was increasingly incomplete. Daphne had a knack of communicating exactly what she needed—in this case, a present mother. Not an empty chair.

The activities coordinator understood perhaps that there were several ways to nurture Daphne, that a careful holding of her was one way, that change and shared community was another. After a very anxious and tearful journey, Daphne, at last in the café, had some respite.

Daphne looks at me, and at the small group of residents she is with. She looks at the woman opposite who is eating much of the cake. "The children are happier. That's what it's all about. It's about the children, about happiness, about care."

I imagined that Daphne saw herself in these "children." She took on the role of the adult in relationship to her peers and of a consultant observing her surroundings. In her commentary, there is a sense of gratitude that the "children" could be cared for.

DOROTHY AND THE ABSENT ORGANIZATIONAL MOTHER

However, the residents didn't always feel cared for. Certainly Dorothy's experience was sometimes one of not being noticed, of being rejected even. Dorothy lived in a larger care home in an affluent area on the outskirts of a town for commuters, situated on the banks of the River Thames. Many residents kept themselves to themselves in the care home, staying in their rooms for much of the day because of a range of nursing needs. Dorothy was a Scottish woman in her late eighties. She had moved to England to be closer to her daughter and grandchildren. Dorothy was seen as troublesome sometimes, becoming agitated when no one responded to her. This was not surprising, since my observations led me to believe that she was regularly not seen or heard, despite the fact that she was always parked up in her wheelchair in a corridor opposite the nurses' station. Dorothy, unlike Daphne, never mentioned her mother or referred to herself as a mother. This absence of maternal reference in itself was striking. Thinking psychoanalytically, I wondered whether this alluded to the general absence of a maternal quality in the care received there.

What I noticed in Dorothy's experience was the way that her relationship with her keyworker, Nancy, a senior care worker, often reminded me of the ambivalent feelings involved in mother-child relating. For Nancy and Dorothy, a mutual disconnection was one of the ways in which their ambivalence communicated itself. In the following vignette, Dorothy is objectified and infantilized. Nancy focuses on Dorothy's appearance more so than on how she might be feeling, as if the outside (presentation) holds more meaning than the inside.

Nancy says that Dorothy's hair is messy, and she will get a comb. She walks into the hair salon and comes back with a comb. She shows it briefly to Dorothy and goes to the back of her head and starts combing. "No, no, no," says Dorothy, grimacing. "That hurts, hurts, hurts."

"But it's messy," says Nancy. "It's nearly done."

"Don't do it, don't, don't," says Dorothy.

Nancy finishes the combing and then looks at Dorothy and says it's better now, smiling. Dorothy shakes her head and quietly looks down. It looks as if tears are forming in her eyes. She brings her head back up and looks ahead.

This vignette symbolized what I came to believe was part of the culture of the home. Encounters involved a form of noticing that was often basic, reductive and surface—teas, biscuits, hair, clothing. The lived experience, the psychic experience in all its hues, was often passed over in much the same way that members of staff walked past Dorothy without acknowledging her.

NO ONE'S MOTHER

Dorothy seemed to represent for the home an overwhelming loneliness. Nancy once talked about Dorothy's daughter while Dorothy sat still in her wheelchair. Without hiding it, Nancy said, "She doesn't come much." This was a double isolation for Dorothy.

The reality of her daughter's infrequent visits was compounded by Nancy's tactless remarks in Dorothy's presence. Dorothy's being there had been forgotten about by both her daughter and by Nancy, who speaks about her situation as if she were not there. Dorothy becomes an absent mother even for her daughter, who rarely keeps her mother in mind.

The care was not always unreceptive. On the contrary, I saw moments when Nancy, particularly, noticed Dorothy, and moments when Dorothy shared her experiences with Nancy. This was played out concretely through the sharing of food. Often Nancy would eat what Dorothy was eating; or would take sips from her drink. However, as a symbolic mother, Nancy could sometimes appear preoccupied and overburdened. Dorothy, in turn, was wounded and would further reject an already absent mothering figure.

Maternal figures (brought forth from the internal spaces of residents' minds or animated through the actual practice of care workers) were present in both sites, some more alive to the textured emotional landscape than others. Generally, though, I experienced an overarching organizational Mother absent particularly to the psychic confusions and pain of both the residents and the care staff, who were tasked with being there on the frontline for many residents who needed them.

CONCLUSION

I wonder now if this absence I perceived could be traced to the difficulty of engaging with people whose worlds can at times be very shaky and who remind us, perhaps, of our shared precariousness as we move through the stages of human life. To be present to this kind of dependency demands of workers and organizations a capacity to recognize the separate centre of subjectivity of the person with dementia (Benjamin 31). It also involves experiencing the self as a fabric made of many different fibres, one of the most primitive being our encounter with a m(O)ther (Ettinger 2) in whom we once dwelled. In other words, we encounter our own dependence. I would argue that the fear that dependence stirs up among us, particularly today—where in many Western cultures there is arguably an overvaluing of robust individualism and independent action—was precisely the reason why Mother, in all her guises, often hid in the shadows of the care homes and, simultaneously, why she was so frequently needed.

WORKS CITED

Benjamin, J. *Like Subjects, Love Objects: Essays on Recognition and Sexual Difference*. Yale Press, 2006.

Bick, E. "Notes on Infant Observation in Psychoanalytic Training." 1964. *Surviving Space: Papers on Infant Observation*, edited by A. Briggs, Tavistock Clinic, 2002, pp. 37-55.

Datler, W., et al. "An Exploration of the Quality of Life in Nursing Homes: The Use of Single Case and Organisational Observation in a Research Project." *Infant Observation*, vol. 12, no. 1, 2009, pp. 63-82.

Dartington, T. *Managing Vulnerability: The Underlying Dynamics of Systems of Care*. Karnac Books, 2010.

Davenhill, R. "Looking into Later Life: Psychodynamic Observation and Old Age." *Psychoanalytic Psychotherapy*, vol. 17, no. 3, 2003, pp. 253-66.

Davenhill, R. "Psychodynamic Observation and Emotional Mapping: A Tool for Continuing Professional Development and Research in Services for Older People." *Quality in Ageing and Older Adults*, vol. 10, no. 1, 2009, pp.32-9.

Ettinger, B. "Matrixial Trans-subjectivity." *Theory, Culture & Society*, vol. 23, 2006, pp. 2-3.

Hinshelwood, RD, and W. Skogstad. *Observing Organisations*. Routledge, 2000.

Larkin, P. *Collected Poems*. Faber, 2003.

Maiello, S. "On Temporal Shapes: The Relation between Primary Rhythmical Experience and the Quality of Mental Links." *Being Alive: Building on the Work of Anne Alvarez*, edited by J. Edwards, Routledge, 2001, pp. 179-95.

Menzies Lyth, Isabel. "The Functions of Social Systems as a Defence Against Anxiety: A Report on a Study of the Nursing Service of a General Hospital." *Human Relations*, vol. 13, 1959, pp. 95-121.

Ogden, T. *The Matrix of the Mind: Object Relations and the Psychoanalytic Dialogue*. Karnac Books, 1992.

Winnicott, DW. *The Maturational Processes and the Facilitating Environment*. Hogarth Press, 1965.

May Breath

Poetics against Canada's Ongoing Settler Colonial Violence toward Indigenous Women and Mothers

SARAH DE LEEUW

1. A BEGINNING. NOT AN INTRODUCTION.

To begin. Oh to begin. To begin.

To begin a life. To be born. Born into this world, a beginning.

Or, to begin writing.

We have all been born. A first breath.

I was born.

You were born.

If we have nothing in common, we have our births. We have birth. To be (like a plant, a tree of leaves and roots and bark seed needle blossom) implanted with a quality. Being born. Breath. Breathe.

I have no children. I have born no one. I have not given birth. I am no mother, nothing mothering.

But I was born. Brought into this world.

We have that in common. Please. Remember this. We have this in common. I am writing to you, implanted rooted leafed landed settler settling a birth, settled. I am writing. Responding to a call:

reconcile, tell a truth, write/right a relationship. Bring this into the world. A writing. What are the qualities of writing?

"I deeply distrust this tool I work with—language," says poet M. NourbeSe Philip (197). Language hides disorder, she continues. It suggests logic where there is no logic; it imposes rationality where there is no rationality. Where there is only a fierce sharp violent effort to dehumanize. The opposite of being born.

Philip is also writing about law. About the language and the spaces of law. About systems of "justice" that "promulgated the non-being of African peoples" (197), that transformed humans into expendable (insured) property. By law. Through language. She could easily be writing about what I am writing. Bodies into materials, a killing, a slaughtering, through words the telling the story. For Philip, the massacre and mass murder of 133 enslaved Africans by the crew of the Dutch slave ship Zong in 1781 (moan, says Philip, call chatter rip mutter howl utter refuse to tell the story   normally   un/tell   a story   beyond telling moan).   Breathe.

In this writing   (moan breath breathesite of being born) an Indigenous mother.   Now absent.

Go beyond language that makes sense. There is no sense.

Think too of Leanne Simpson's "caged knowledge" (380). Yes, she is writing about Indigenous Knowledge, about land protocol ecology environment knowledge, but she is writing about language: "when knowledge is made into a text [its interpretation becomes locked] in a cognitive box ... stripped of its dynamism and its fluidity" (380).

Now remember   we are born.   I was born. You   were born. Remember this again. And think of the muscly flesh and blood fluid skinland bodyland humanplace and breath breath pulse membrane pull water contraction (no matter how or where or what form, so many forms of birth we are not born of one mother) that surrounded you upon birth. Think of this locked. In language. In a courtroom.

    Caged. Skinland bodyland humanplace mother birthsite. Bottled. Pelvis. Birthsite. Caged.

Let us think together of Cindy Gladue. Mother of three. Mother. Birth. Born. Born of Donna McLeod. Born. Into this world. Breathing. Implanted.

2. THE IMPOSSIBLE. AN (UN)TELLING. A SECOND, MORE-THAN VIOLENCE, A COURT. LAW.

Off.   The Yellowhead   (1825   Pierre Bostonais is Tete –head-
    Jaune – yellow - a fur trader he hides his pelts, pelts, all
    the skins stealing trading skins skins map of skins hiding
    skins the man has hidden his skins the highway hiding skins
    already skinning and hiding has begun, men on land that
    is not their own a highway of tears)
Highway.   22 June 2011.   The Yellowhead Inn (high-
way-side   motel).
    Bath. Of. Blood.   Edmonton. Yellowhead
yellow head   man truckingOntarioman calls 911   f r i g g i n ',
friggin', friggin'   "I woke up"
    Don't   want my wife   knowin'
skinskinskinskinskin yellowheadinn   hidingskinsbathtubblood
   friggin'   I'ma truckin'man woke up yellowheadhighway-
highwayswheremengettokillIndigenouswomeninyellowheadin-
bathtubcallin'iamiamiam i am a furniture man   partyingman
yellowhead party   don't know no girl am scared shitless got
kids got kids got kids don't know her poked gut her partying I got
kids   scared   scared   scaredshitless here.

    …

Bar. Room. Bag. Video. Bath. Bled. Out. Gut. Towel. Wiping. Trash. Can. Rough. Fist. Knife. Fist. Knife. Fist. Knife. Fist. Specimen. Evidence. Knife. Fist. Knife.

...

R *v* Barton (language)

...

Mothers are absent here. Rendered pelvic. Language.

...

R *v* Barton

...

What is the *v* again?   Versus. Beyond verses.   V   ag   ai   n
versus again andagainandagain and again verses again.
Nothing makes sense.

non/sense versus verses

...

co   u   rt
                     d   o   cke   t
        reg   i
stry
                                    Ed mon   ton
Her Majesty the Queen Respondent (Appellant)
~~Bradley Barton~~ Respondent (Respondent)
Medical examiner
                                    pro se   cut   or
Own defense   own defense   own defense   owndefense
OWN defense
Forensic
Consent
Law of consent
Autopsy
Thirty-six years old
Cindy
Three daughters
Cheyanne Kelly

Brandy Sierra
Brianne Nicole
Mother
Donna McLeod

Vaginal tissue

Evidence

       tr   i   al

       sha   r   p   ob   j   e   ct

Torn

mother mother mother mother mother mother mother mother
mother mother

...

Barton
Acquitted
First Degree Murder
Acquitted
Manslaughter

...

Appeal
Legal Errors
Before Deliberations

...

Indigenous mother Indigenous mother Indigenous mother
Indigenous mother Indigenous mother Indigenous mother
Indigenous mother Indigenous mother Indigenous mother
Indigenous mother Indigenous mother Indigenous mother

...

We are all born. Breath.
...

He states he went to sleep. He states he woke up. He woke up.

...

Appeal. Breath. Appeal.

...

March 2016 Docket: 1503-0091-A

– and –
Women's Legal Education and Action Fund Inc. and
Institute for the Advancement of Aboriginal Women
Applicants (Proposed Interveners)

– reasons –
The Honourable Mr. Justice Ronald Berger

[1] Following a trial in the Court of Queen's Bench the respondent
was found not guilty of causing the death of Cindy Gladue and
thereby committing first-degree murder contrary to s. 235(1) of
the *Criminal Code*.
[2] The Crown has appealed. The grounds of appeal as framed by
the appellant are the following:

She will never return
She was born
She is more
We breathe
She is a mother
She will always be
If there is sky and forest

Someone has the right to an ocean
We are obligated
That which is always colonial
Somewhere there are prairies
We cannot be this
A calling
We will all be, we all are, broken
Because of this one
A highway kills
Answers
Such further and other good grounds as counsel may advise.

[4] I have reviewed the case law setting out the considerations that govern applications for intervener status in criminal cases. They include the following:

More than
Not enough
Tremors
Tears
Mothers
Women
Our bodies
All our bodies
History

Whether the proposed intervener has a real, substantial, and iden-tifiable interest in the subject matter of the proceedings.

[5] Some judges have opined that it is very unusual for the court to consider interventions in criminal appeals. The accused/respondent was represented by a lawyer who had been admitted to the Alberta bar a mere two years earlier in 2007.

[13] I have come to the conclusion upon a consideration of all of the factors set out earlier in

That which is greater than all of us

The clouds
The soil
The teeth we see when she smiles
The joy
Everyone's soft skin
Roads built without reason
Repeating waves
Particles of light
People taking what is not theirs
Unsolved slaughtering

these Reasons for Decision that the three judges of the Court of
Appeal who will sit in judgment on the appeal ... [and] I see no
prejudice to the respondent, provided that the submissions of the
interveners are confined to the proposed joint factum.

I grant leave to intervene to

Speak
Scream
Sob
Moan
Mourn
Have rights
Call upon the moon
Know a truth
Reconcile
Write
Feel as a family might
Gain equality

that extent only. The application to make oral submissions not
exceeding 20 minutes.

[14] The joint factum of the interveners shall be filed forthwith.

Reasons filed at Edmonton, Alberta
this 8th day of March, 2016

3. WRITING BREATHING, BREATHING AGAIN

may   a river meet your breath   may   calm
may your mother's   palm   greet   you   may all   snow
may   some path   breath   may the sky   may
a sweetness sweetgrassmay your daughters   find   may a
coolness   may the wind   may many   breath
breath   may
                    all the birds of flight
breath may your family   may no tears   breath   may
some calm   may silk   may   summer   mayabright
bright spark   breath
may every word gentle   may each part of your body   may
the day you
          were born may every wound may every wonder   may
a blanket   breath may gifts   may what is new   may
what you want   may the ground may moss may song may
ocean may fields of wheat may the moon may sands may the first
taste of a ripe berry may a seed may mist may crisp frost may
ripe fruit may fast fast wolves may streams of fish may gardens
may a kindness may a fighting chance breath breath may clay
may downiness may clouds may horizon may hawks' calling may
aurora borealis may the moment between sleep and awakening
may blue may green may yellow may morning may breath may
breath may living may no wanting may starfish may a daisy may
salt may lakes may a glow may air may leaves
          may breath may breath may breath   may you be
inhaling   may you be whole may the road may all time may
sleep may daughters   may women   may rest   may
breath   may breath   may a learning may breath

4. BEYOND CONCLUSION

Because Cindy Gladue is a mother.
Because she has a mother.
Because.
We are all born.
May breath.

WORKS CITED

Philip, Marlene NourbeSe, and Setaey Adamu Boateng. *Zong!:As Told to the Author by Setaey Adamu Boateng.* Mercury Press, 2008.

Simpson, Leanne R. "Anticolonial Strategies for the Recovery and Maintenance of Indigenous Knowledge." *The American Indian Quarterly*, vol. 28, no. 3, 2005, pp. 373-84.

R. v. Barton, ABCA 68, *CanLII*, 2016, canlii.ca/t/gnmjw. Accessed 29 June 2017.

My Nehiyaw Mother

RANDY LUNDY

I AM GOING TO SPEAK a little about my mother: how she was there, then was not there, and then how she was once again.

I am looking at a black-and-white photograph of a dark-haired, dark-skinned woman holding a one-year-old child under the arms, as the child stands on a Formica tabletop; the white walls of the kitchen are bare. No one else is in the frame of the photo, and I do not know who took it. I know the woman in the picture is my mother and the child is me. I know this because before mailing the picture many years ago, my older sister, Dorothy, wrote on the back "This is Mom and you."

While growing up, I knew nothing of my mother—not her name, whether she was alive or dead, where (if she was alive) she lived, or what she looked like. I could have passed her on the street and would not have recognized her. I certainly had no idea what her voice might sound like or what it might feel like to be held by her. I had absolutely no memory of her, and she was not a subject that my father and I ever discussed. The absence and the silence were complete.

The absence of a mother and the silence that surrounded it were simply facts of my life that I had to accept in order to survive.

The only time the subject of my mother (and siblings) was broached was when I was nineteen and filling out the personal history section of a Canadian Armed Forces application. Rather embarrassed, I had to ask my father for the names of my mother and any siblings, along with their birthdates. It was the one and only time we ever spoke of this past. He provided the information as best he could. I copied it onto the form, and anything else we could have said on the matter was never spoken. My father has now been dead for twenty-six years.

I was born in northern Manitoba, in Thompson in 1967, the only son of Elmer Lundy, a man of Norwegian and Irish descent, and Marguerite Bighetty, a Cree or Cree-Scots woman, depending on who is telling the story. My father's parents farmed near Smeaton, Saskatchewan, which is on Highway 55 east of Prince Albert, and he grew up on the family homestead. My mother's parents worked a trapline near the community of Brochet, Manitoba, on the north-eastern shore of Reindeer Lake. She had her first team of dogs, three of them, at the age of eight. Nevertheless, my mother was never recognized as a status Indian under the terms of the Indian Act, since until 1985 children born to Indigenous women and non-Indigenous men were not recognized as Status Indians.

The policy was both sexist and racist, since non-Indigenous women who married Indigenous men immediately gained status, as did the children of such unions. Presumably, the intent of such policies was that over time, there would be fewer status Indians to whom the federal government would have fiduciary and treaty obligations. In the case of my immediate family, the policy was having the intended effect, since my mother—and hence I and my siblings—were not recognized as Status Indians.

Details are foggy for me, and silences are dogged, but sometime around 1970, when I was three years old, my father left my mother and took me with him. I was his only child, as my five half-brothers and sisters were born of two different fathers in the years before my father and mother met. I have learned since that my father beat my mother badly enough to put her in the hospital, and, presumably, this precipitated their separation. I have vague memories of being left at my aunt and uncle's home in Hudson Bay, Saskatchewan, while my father headed west, to British Columbia, to look for work. I am not sure if I remember this or have simply filled in the memory after being told the story of my mother arriving at my aunt and uncle's doorstep with an RCMP escort to take me back to Thompson. At some point after that, my father must have taken me back once again. The way my mother tells it now, she thought it was for the best, since she thought my father might be able to give me a better life. Perhaps she made the right decision, as she was alone with four other children to raise (my oldest brother was raised by our maternal grandparents), but knowing the kind of man my father was, I am not sure she had much choice in who would raise me.

Hence, no doubt at my father's insistence, I was separated from my mother and my three sisters and two brothers for the next twenty-plus years and had no contact with or knowledge of them until after my father's death in 1990, when he was fifty-one. I was raised by my father, surrounded by much of his family—my aunts and uncles and cousins—in Hudson Bay, Saskatchewan. I was raised in complete ignorance of my maternal ancestors and my Indigenous heritage. However, my dark eyes, hair, and darker skin tone relative to my Norwegian and Irish paternal relations marked me as different from and other than. Perhaps this was clear to everyone except me. As with most children, I did not want to be recognizably and identifiably different; I simply wanted to fit in, to be accepted. As such, whenever my physical differences led others to single me out, it was a painful and embarrassing experience.

Furthermore, my physical characteristics also marked me as different from most of the other people in the community. Hudson Bay owed and still owes its existence to the boreal forest. Forestry is the primary industry, and its population was, and still is, primarily Caucasian and Euro-Canadian. In the late 1970s and early 1980s, there was a small number of other Indigenous students in the school, many of whom came from a smaller, nearby community, called Reserve, tucked away in the bush off the highway south of Hudson Bay. Unsurprisingly, these students never quite seemed to fit in and didn't exactly excel in school. Looking back, I am not surprised that most of them dropped out of school and out of sight as soon as they were able to do so. At the time, I had no understanding of the circumstances for the seeming disappearance of these students and didn't have the tools to link their disappearances with the disappearance of my mother and siblings from my own life.

Although I do not remember overt racism toward Indigenous

students in school (perhaps a blindness born of some privilege), they were marked not only by physical differences but also by economic indicators, such as clothing, by speech accent and patterns, and by geography, as they lived in a tiny, isolated community hidden away in the bush. In other words, they were socially and economically marginalized in relation to the community in which I lived. Even though I too was marked as physically different, I did not share with them other indicators of difference. Without anything approaching a full understanding of how or why these students were different, I saw them through my own colonized vision: I saw them as dark—usually darker in skin tone than me—poor, dirty, and somehow vaguely threatening. Rather than identifying with these students, I rejected them as others did because of my own ignorance about my past and personal history. I cannot say for sure but perhaps when I looked at those students, something in me recognized my own difference reflected, and I wanted absolutely nothing to do with being different.

I remember a particular incident from childhood that, on the surface, seems insignificant but that wounded me deeply. One day on the playground at school I became engaged in a verbal sparring match with one of my classmates, a girl on whom I had had a crush for several years. As the bell rang summoning us back into the school, she shouted at me: "At least my parents didn't abandon me to be raised by strangers." In my body, my chest and gut, I can still feel the acidic tone of her voice and the deep emptiness I felt upon hearing her words. Although I found her comment deeply troubling and well beyond the range of my understanding, I was vaguely, perhaps intuitively, aware that her words must be related to the facts of my eye, hair, and skin colours that identified me as different from my father and his family in ways I could not articulate. I was hurt, embarrassed, and confused by the comment because it cut to the heart of my own ignorance of who I was and where I had come from.

I moved to Saskatoon, Saskatchewan, to attend university in 1987. My father died in 1990; and in April of 1991, I was rereading *Richard III* in preparation for a final exam in a Shakespeare class when the telephone rang. My roommate answered and then called me to the phone. A voice on the line asked, "Hello? Hello? Is this Randy Lundy? Were you born in Thompson, Manitoba, on 8 November1967?" Then the voice said, "You probably don't remember me, but I remember you. We haven't talked for twenty years. This is your sister Dorothy." Suddenly twenty-plus years of silence was broken. From my sister, I learned that for all of those years, people of whom I knew nothing, my mother and siblings, had thought of, wondered about, missed, and loved me. I learned that my mother had cried and laughed as she spoke to her five children about her sixth, her lost baby boy. I learned that my family had long been aware of my whereabouts but had been waiting for the right time and had been summoning the courage to contact me. For my mother, the time and courage had not yet come. She was frightened of what she might or might not say to me, and frightened of how I may or may not respond.

A week after speaking with my sister, I was still stunned, in a state of shock, and had cried both inwardly and outwardly. Then a large, padded, yellow-brown envelope arrived in the mail. Inside was my birth certificate, a lengthy letter from my sister, and a number of photographs with printing on the backs to guide me among unrecognizable faces and into an unfamiliar past—my own. I am looking at one of those photographs now. On the back of the photograph, in my sister's printing, it says, "This is Mom and you." After another week had passed, my mother finally worked up the courage to call me. I remember little of what was said, but I do remember these words from my mother: "I never forgot you, my boy. I have always thought about you and loved you even though we could not be together." What I remember just as clearly was simply listening to the sound of her voice, my mind racing wildly and incoherently, and the repetition of two phrases pulsing, beating inside me like a drumbeat: *my boy*, my mother, *my boy*, my mother, *my boy*, my mother. My life had changed irrevocably.

A short time after the events I have just described, I was talking with a friend whom I had met shortly after my father and I moved from Quesnel, British Columbia, to Hudson Bay in the mid-1970s. He had been a friend for approximately twenty years at that point. I told him that my sister and then my mother had re-established contact with me. Upon hearing this, he asked a question that stunned me. He asked if I had ever found out who my real father was. I was stunned because I had been raised by my father, and now a friend who had known me for twenty years was asking about who my real father might have been. Suddenly that acerbic comment on the playground years before made complete sense. Although no one had ever said anything to me, aside from once in a heated playground exchange, it was obvious that at least some of my peers had always assumed that because my physical appearance was different from that of my father and his family, I could not possibly be one of them. Apparently, in the eyes of some of the residents of Hudson Bay, I must have been adopted.

In light of my own ignorance, that of some of my peers was understandable. More than once over the years, I have had people suggest to me that in some ways I grew up as if I were an adoptee. It's true. I grew up in ignorance of half of my family history, and with the shame and confusion that that ignorance—and a silence enforced by my father—caused. Physical characteristics inherited from my Cree mother set me apart from my father and paternal relatives, and all of this caused some to suspect I was not really who I seemed to be. Finally, many years later, I was reunited with my mother and siblings. So, yes, in some ways I have journeyed a path similar to that of adoptees. I think of the thousands of Indigenous children who were torn from their homes, families, communities, and cultures by violent racist policies that assumed Indigenous peoples were unfit to raise their own children. It was violence, too, that took me away from my mother and took my mother away from me, but all such violence must be overcome, and it my case, it has been.

In the summer of 2015, I visited my father's grave for the first time since I buried him. Twenty-five years had passed. The spring of 2016 marked twenty-five years since my phone rang and I spoke first with my sister and then a short time later with my mother. The events I have shared here, which took place from the late 1960s to the mid-1990s, seem to me as much mythology as personal history. It has been a long and fascinating road, an uncertain journey. For the past twenty years, I have taught Indigenous literatures at the post-secondary level. I have learned much from study, and I have learned much from my Mom and siblings and from many other teachers along the way—professors, students, friends, and Elders. I am approaching the age of fifty. My father now has been physically absent from my life for longer than he was present in it; my mother now has been present in my life for longer than she was absent from it. When we speak, she still says, "My boy," and I love that—a warmth and fullness where there used to be a wind-swept emptiness; and my heart-drum still sings "My mother, my mother, my mother...."

This morning, I attended a pipe ceremony. Tomorrow, I will attend a sweat ceremony. There will be drumming and singing and praying.

I am going to leave you with three poems I have written about my Mom, and then it will be done. Thank you for hearing.

"For My Mother" (from *Under the Night Sun*, 1999)

A sky heavy with clouds
a bough burdened with snow

your tongue bends
to touch the frozen earth

the tracks of small animals have led you
into this sheltered place
you kill and roast their bodies
over a slow, green fire

when your hunger is fed
you suck marrow from thin bones
warm icicles in your mouth

now, perhaps, you can say
how memory lives in the bones
how it is possible

to swallow blood and marrow
to speak from this quiet centre

"The Night of My Conception"
(from *The Gift of the Hawk*, 2004)

You stood on a long finger of stone
pointing itself into the lake
drawing your attention to the water
rising and falling on driftwood shores;

your face was smooth
deerhide stretched on a drum
a few bloodstains on the skin
birthmarks on the belly of a son;

your hair, long and fluid
would later become brittle moss
abandoned for the winter
on the south facing
spines of the trees;

your face would carry
the marks of the land that bore it
a country of rock, sheared
by wind and rain, grooved by ice
a few scars from the hand
of a man who loved you;

in those grooves gathered bits of soil
where seeds settled and began
to sing their green prayers to the sky;

soon bark and leaves
growing from the inside out
memory ringed around itself;

that night my father's hands gripped you
the hands of a miner on the thin wrist of a pick—

the hands of a man

who brought food to you and your children
when your husband was nowhere to be found
raising his whiskey-filled glass to the night, to a friend
to some woman who was not you—

and the stone inside your body fell
like a full, winter moon

and a new season
you had no names for
was born.

"January" (from *Blackbird Song,* 2017)

The dead of winter
I am thinking
Of my mother

She exists for me
The way the owl

Perches
On black spruce
Backlit by streetlight
Grey against night sky

Just before taking flight.

Remembering the Mothers of the Stolen Children

A Discussion of the Representation of Mothers in Jane Harrison's Play *Stolen*

EMMA DALTON

THE INDIGENOUS AUSTRALIAN MOTHERS within Jane Harrison's play *Stolen* are depicted as strong women and powerful memories. Harrison's central characters are stolen children, and their memories of their mothers provide a source of hope for them long after they are taken. Harrison's stolen children are written to be representative of Australia's Stolen Generations. When I refer to the Stolen Generation, I write in the plural: I write of the Stolen Generations, because there was not one Stolen Generation of Indigenous people in Australia; rather, there were many. Australian scholar and public intellectual Robert Manne states, "From the late nineteenth century to the late 1960s ... Australian governments, as a practice and as a policy, removed part-Aboriginal children from their mothers, parents, families and communities, often by force" (53). He makes reference to *Bringing Them Home* (1997), the Report of the National Inquiry into the Separation of Aboriginal and Torres Strait Islander Children from Their Families, and notes that the number of Indigenous children taken from their families is difficult to estimate accurately. Manne writes, "[The report] suggests that somewhere between one in three and one in ten Aboriginal children were separated from their mothers during these years" (53). The representation of the stolen children's mothers as women who mourn for and do not forget their children provides an important rewriting of dominant narratives, as the playwright explains in "My Journey through *Stolen*" (65-6). Furthermore, live performances of *Stolen* have enacted a form of commemoration for the Stolen Generations, and the play-text of *Stolen* offers a script for further acts of remembrance (Casey 217).

Harrison's play *Stolen* premiered in the Beckett Theatre at the CUB Malthouse, Playbox Theatre Company on 21 October 1998 as part of the Melbourne International Festival. It received a standing ovation at its 1998 Melbourne premiere and saw sold-out seasons across Australia (Enoch vii). *Stolen* has been staged in the United Kingdom, Hong Kong, and Japan, and it has had readings in Canada and New York (*Stolen* i). Through the vehicle of theatre, Harrison has shared the stories of the Stolen Generations with thousands across the globe. Furthermore, the Indigenous mothers within Harrison's play-text are represented as engaging in maternal practices before their children are removed and also as endeavouring to engage in maternal practices after their removal.

The Indigenous mothers within *Stolen* may be understood to undertake maternal practices and to engage in maternal thinking despite their separation from their children (Ruddick 17). Furthermore, this chapter argues that the Indigenous mother characters and their children resist national and institutional operations of forgetting to remember one another, despite institutions persistently telling them to forget (Connerton 59).

VERBATIM THEATRE

Stolen is a verbatim play. Deirdre Heddon describes verbatim theatre as "a form of theatre which places interviews with people at the heart of its process" (127). Of verbatim theatre Heddon states, "Though there are wide variations in terms of form and practices ... many productions do share a dramaturgical structure. Typically, they create a collage that enables multiple points of view, represented through multiple voices, but anchor this to a single or central storyline or thematic..." (Heddon 128). *Stolen* has a central thematic and common location. Harrison's central characters are representative of Australia's Stolen Generations. The play depicts its central characters at multiple stages of their lives. Although there is not a single or central storyline, the stories of the five stolen children share significant commonalities, and all of the central characters are, at different points in the play, together in a children's home. The play-text does not follow a linear narrative. Rather, to adopt Heddon's terminology, it creates a "collage" (128) of multiple stories.

Many of the experiences represented within the play-text of *Stolen* are inspired by real experiences. Spectators who watch *Stolen* participate in the remembrance of real and traumatic events. Harrison identifies lawyer and activist Antoinette Braybrook as the primary researcher in *Stolen's* developmental process. Furthermore, she states that Braybrook "fed [her] a stream of books and documents" and provided her with "a conduit to the community" (Harrison, "My Journey through Stolen" 64). According to Harrison, Braybrook had contacts that she did not have, yet Harrison also listened to the stories of stolen children and their families. These stories directly affected the play-text of *Stolen*. Harrison states, "[She] heard of a mother who, having seen her child bundled into the welfare's big, black car without a word said to her, was paralyzed with grief and stood in the rain unable to move or speak" (66). "[This story]", Harrison writes, "became the basis of two vignettes in the play for the character of Shirley" (66). Hence, when spectators observe Shirley's memories of her removal, they are observing an experience which was lived.

The use of symbolic objects is another characteristic of verbatim theatre that is significant within *Stolen*. The stolen children's beds are an element of set that remains consistent throughout the play. The beds link the children with one another and with a common location—the children's home. The beds remain onstage for the entirety of the production. At times, the beds are used to symbolize places outside of the institution of the children's home, for example, a pier or a jail cell.

MATERNAL PRACTICES

I propose that the Indigenous mother characters in *Stolen* undertake maternal practices and that through their engagement in acts of maternal work, they are represented as being responsive to the requirements of their children and the demands of society, despite their separation from "the reality of a biological child in a particular social world" (Ruddick 17).

The maternal practices in *Stolen* can be understood by examining Sara Ruddick's work. Ruddick describes preservative love as an action of mother work, which is performed in response to a demand made by a child, the demand for preservation. For Ruddick, preservative love is a maternal practice that is chosen. Of "mother-love," Ruddick states, "What we are pleased to call 'mother-love' is intermixed with hate, sorrow, impatience, resentment, and despair; thought-provoking ambivalence is a hallmark of mothering" (68). It is apparent that, for Ruddick, mother-love is complex and contains both positive and negative emotions. Hence, a mother engages in preservative love as an act of will.

Ruddick further describes the maternal practice of nurturing. She states, "To foster growth is to nurture a child's developing spirit" (82). She defines the term "spirit," in this context, as "whatever in a child is lively, purposive, and responsive" (82). Ruddick positions the mother as the individual responsible for the nurturing of a child's "developing spirit" (82). I suggest that the Indigenous mothers within *Stolen* foster their children's growth when they are with them and seek to do so when they are separated from them.

Ruddick's third maternal practice is the practice of training. Two ideas are at the root of her discussion of training: "first, children's natures are hospitable to goodness; and second, maternal work is potentially a work of conscience" (103). According to Ruddick, children need to be trained "to be the kind of [people] others accept and whom the mothers themselves can actively appreciate" (104). However, she identifies "two struggles within maternal practice" (103). These struggles, she states, "[are] between inauthenticity and conscience and between domination and educative control" (103). Although Ruddick's first two maternal practices (preservative love and nurturance) respond to the demands or requirements of a child, her third maternal practice (training) responds to the demands of society or the mother's social group. In *Stolen*, the Indigenous mothers may not have the ability to respond to their children's immediate needs; however, they endeavor to respond to the needs that they perceive their children have. Furthermore, they manifest a comprehension that their children must learn to function in a society that has strict rules with which they may not be familiar. Despite their separation from their children, the children's mothers try to guide their children to obey these rules, this is evident in the letters which Jimmy's mother writes.

REPRESSIVE ERASURE AS THE CONDEMNATION OF MEMORY

Paul Connerton describes "forgetting" as an act that society considers a failing, whereas "remembering" is considered a virtue (59). According to Connerton, at least seven types of forgetting exist: "repressive erasure; prescriptive forgetting; forgetting that is constitutive in the formation of a new identity; structural amnesia; forgetting as annulment; forgetting as planned obsolescence; forgetting as humiliated silence" (59). Repressive erasure, as it is manifested within the play-text of *Stolen*, will be discussed in this chapter.

One phrase that Connerton uses to describe forgetting as repressive erasure is "*damnatio memoriae*" or "the condemnation of memory" (60). Of this type of forgetting Connerton writes the following:

> As the condemnation of memory (*damnatio memoriae*), it was inscribed in Roman criminal and constitutional law as a punishment applied to rulers and other powerful persons who at their death or after a revolution were declared to be "enemies of the state": images of them were destroyed, statues of them were razed to the ground, and their names were removed from inscription, with the explicit purpose of casting all memory into oblivion. (Connerton 60)

In this context, repressive erasure is enacted as the condemnation of memory. With the death of the individual, the individual's memory is condemned to death, *damnatio memoriae*. This punishment seems unspeakably harsh. The individual is condemned to die and all memory of her is condemned to death along with her. Images destroyed, statues dismantled, names erased, the individuals condemned to death and to *damnatio memoriae* are wiped from the earth and no whisper of their existence is permitted to remain.

In *Stolen*, Jimmy's mother, Nancy Wajurri, sends clothes and letters to Jimmy. These actions can be understood as mother work.

Jimmy's mother writes that Jimmy's father is unwell and that they are poor, but she has also knitted Jimmy a pair of warm socks. Although Nancy is not with Jimmy, she knows that he requires clothes to keep warm in winter. She sends clothes not only because she knows he needs them but also because she wants to care for him and wants him to know that she cares for him. She sends letters because she wants to express her love and to instruct him (or train him) regarding how to behave so that he can survive in his new environment. The clothes and letters that Nancy sends indicate that she is attempting to engage in Ruddick's maternal practices of preservative love and training. However, the letters and clothes are shut away in a filing cabinet. Each letter is deposited within, and the filing cabinet is slammed shut. The matron in the children's home pronounces Jimmy's mother dead. Although she does not destroy the evidence of Nancy's attempts at contacting him, she locks it away, and Jimmy's memory of his mother is condemned to death (*damnatio memoriae*). Nancy attempts to engage in the maternal practices of preservative love and training, but the authority figures at the children's home attempt to facilitate the operation of forgetting which Connerton refers to as repressive erasure. When Jimmy is grown and free (albeit temporarily), a man in a bar tells him that his mother is alive. He finds it hard to believe because he has been told that she is dead so many times and he has no knowledge of her letters or her knitting. However, the man gifts Jimmy with the knowledge that he has a living mother. He says that he looks like his mother and that she has been looking for him.

MAN: He's the one she's been looking for, I bet. Hey bros, you here to see ya mum? (*Stolen* 27)

Nancy's search for her son does not go unnoticed. Decades after his removal, she is still searching for him, and the man whom Jimmy meets in a bar knows this. Outside of the children's home, the authorities cannot shut Nancy and her acts away in a filing cabinet. The script suggests that the two arrange to meet. In scene thirty two, titled "What Do You Do?" (*Stolen* 29), the stage directions state "JIMMY and his MOTHER, NANCY (the actor playing SHIRLEY), each speak alternatively, but without hearing the other. SANDY, RUBY and ANNE are singing 'Happy Birthday to You' quietly" (*Stolen* 29). The scene suggests that the two have learned about one another somehow and that they have arranged to meet. Both are very nervous. Neither knows what the other has been through. Nancy does not know that Jimmy has experienced neglect and abuse. Jimmy does not know that Nancy has sent him clothes and letters. Nancy takes twenty-six presents from a box, one for each year since Jimmy was taken. The stage directions state that they "represent all of the love she was not able to give her son" (*Stolen* 30). At the end of the scene, Jimmy's mother collapses and dies. Nancy dies before she is able to give Jimmy a single gift, and he never sees his mother again after he is taken from her, and when he is told—in prison—that his mother is dead, he takes his life by hanging himself. He writes a suicide note, part of which is addressed to his mother. And like the letters his mother sent to him, his letter is shut away in a filing cabinet. The filing cabinet is slammed shut once more, yet in death, it seems that Jimmy and his mother are freed from the control of the white system. The repressive erasure that the authority figures in the children's home attempt to enforce does not succeed in forcing Jimmy or his mother to forget each other. They continue to remember.

Nancy's maternal practices are also noted by those around her—so much so that a man whom Jimmy meets in a bar twenty-six years after his removal can say that he is the one she has been looking for. It is evident that the authority figures within the children's home attempt to facilitate repressive erasure and that through her acts of mother work, Nancy resists the institution's attempts to make her forget. Jimmy also resists their lies. Although he does not get to meet his mother as an adult, he learns that she did search for him and she loved him.

REPRESSIVE ERASURE AS THE ERASURE OF LANGUAGE

Connerton offers a second context for repressive erasure in his discussion of the French Revolution:

> The French Revolution sought to eliminate all remnants of the ancient regime in a similar way [to the condemnation of memory]; monarchical titles and titles of nobility were abolished; the polite forms of address, "Monsieur,"

"Madame," and "Mademoiselle" were eliminated; the polite distinction between two forms of the second person, "vous" (formal) and "tu" (informal) was supposed to be forgotten; and the names of historical provinces of France—Burgundy, Provence, and so on—were consigned to oblivion. (Connerton 60)

In this context, repressive erasure was enacted to force forgetting and to erase language.

This form of erasure is emphasized by a single line of dialogue within Harrison's play-text, which reveals a cruel and racist rule within the children's home: "But you're not allowed to say that..." (*Stolen* 10). Shirley makes this statement in response to Sandy speaking in an Indigenous language, Yorta Yorta. He says the word "yurringa" (*Stolen* 10), which the stage directions specify is "local dialect for 'sun'" (*Stolen* 10). Shirley's statement shows that the children are not permitted to speak in Indigenous languages. In order for languages to be remembered, they must be spoken. In this scene, repressive erasure is manifested as the forced forgetting of language. The children know that they will be punished if they speak in their native languages. Although this scene is evidence of an atrocious rule in the children's home, it also shows that Sandy remembers what he was taught prior to removal from his family.

Sandy tells the other children at the children's home two Indigenous stories. The first is his story of "the big bad Mungee" (*Stolen* 10), which he says his grandfather told him. The second is his story of the "red sands" (*Stolen* 10), which his mother told him. Within the play-text, it is evident that Sandy was cared for by a network of individuals, including his mother and his extended family. Jane Moore and Lynette Riley state, "Prior to contact [colonization] the kinship systems which operated across Australia provided complex and sophisticated reciprocal relationships based upon both biological and kinship lines of descent" (176). According to Moore and Riley, "in these social systems the role of 'mother' was performed by not only the birth mother, but also those women who were at the same 'kinship' level as the birth mother" (176). Sandy's memories of his life prior to removal include (but are not limited to) multiple members of his family: his mum, his cousin, his aunt, his aunty, his uncle, and his grandfather. Moore and Riley discuss "the ways in which the notion of being a 'good' Aboriginal mother is uniquely linked to Aboriginal kinship systems" (175), and within *Stolen*, Sandy learns from, and is cared for, by many members of his family. Ruddick acknowledges that not only birth mothers have the capacity to mother; she posits that even men can engage in mother work. Ruddick states, "whatever difference might exist between female and male mothers, there is no reason to believe that one sex rather than the other is more capable of doing maternal work" (41).

Although Shirley tells Sandy that he is not allowed to speak in Indigenous languages, Sandy still remembers the language he learned prior to removal. He remembers the stories that he was told. Sandy is the only central character who tells Indigenous stories; he is the only central character who speaks in an Indigenous language. The telling of stories and the teaching of Indigenous languages can be understood to be indicative of the maternal practice of training. Furthermore, the telling of stories and the teaching of Indigenous languages performed by a mother (or parental figure) to a child is indicative of Toni Morrison's "African-American custom of culture bearing" (O'Reilly 133). Andrea O'Reilly states, "Toni Morrison, in a manner similar to the model developed by Sara Ruddick, positions motherwork as a practice committed to meeting specific tasks" (133). However, Morrison "[amplifies] the aim of 'training' ... to include the African American custom of cultural bearing..." (133). Morrison's concept of cultural bearing is evident within *Stolen* through the stories and language Sandy remembers. Sandy is a son. However, he received stories and language from the "motherline" (O'Reilly 118) and from his grandfather. Within the context of Naomi Lowinsky's concept of "the motherline," O'Reilly describes black, African American mothers as "cultural bearers and tradition keepers" (118). She proposes that "motherline stories, made available to daughters through the female oral tradition, unite mothers and daughters and connect them to their motherline" (119). She argues that "in [the context of] African American society the motherline represents ancestral memory, traditional values of African American culture ... Black mothers pass on the teachings of the motherline to each successive generation through the maternal function of cultural bearing" (119). Although O'Reilly and Morrison speak about African American mothers and the motherline specifically refers to the passing on of culture from a mother to her daughters, I would suggest that Sandy's knowledge of Indigenous stories and Indigenous languages can be understood within the context of culture bearing. He has received culture (language and stories) from his mother and extended family, and he bears that culture. He remembers, despite the threat of punishment. Sandy appears determined to remember the stories and language that he has received from his family; hence, he tells those stories and he speaks in Indigenous languages in order to remember them.

The Indigenous mothers and the stolen children within Harrison's play resist national and institutional operations of forgetting to remember one another. *Stolen* tells the stories of the Stolen Generations through the mode of theatre, enabling spectators to both see and hear their stories. By representing the mothers of the stolen children as individuals endeavouring to engage in maternal practices both prior to and after the removal of their children, Harrison presents them as being aware of the requirements of their children and responsive to those requirements. Furthermore, by representing the operations of forgetting at work within the institution of the children's home, Harrison illuminates the resistance of the Indigenous mothers and their stolen children, refusing to forget.

Note: Some portions of this essay have already been published under the name Emma Hughes (my maiden name) in Outskirts: Feminisms along the Edge, *vol. 33, 2015 pp. 1-17.*

WORKS CITED

Casey, Edward S. *Remembering: A Phenomenological Study.* Indiana University Press, 1987.

Connerton, Paul. "Seven Types of Forgetting." *Memory Studies,* vol. 1, no. 1, 2008, pp. 59-71.

Enoch, Wesley. "Making History: Directing the First Production of *Stolen.*" *Stolen.* By Jane Harrison. 1998. Currency Press, 2007, pp. vii-xi.

Harrison, Jane. "Author's Note." *Stolen*. By Jane Harrison. 1998. Currency Press, 2007, pp. xiii-xiv.

Harrison, Jane. *Stolen*. 1998. Currency Press, 2007.

Harrison, Jane. "My Journey through *Stolen*." *Just Words? Australian Authors Writing for Justice*, edited by Bernadette Brennan, Queensland University Press, 2008, pp. 62-75.

Heddon, Deirdre. *Autobiography and Performance: Performing Selves*. Palgrave McMillan, 2008.

Hughes, Emma. "Maternal Practice and Maternal Presence in Jane Harrison's *Stolen*." *Outskirts: Feminisms along the Edge*, vol. 33, 2015 pp. 1-17.

Manne, Robert. "The Stolen Generations." *Quadrant*, vol. 42, no. 1-2, 1998, pp. 53-63.

Moore, Jane and Lynette Riley. "Aboriginal Mother Yarns." *The Good Mother: Contemporary Motherhoods in Australia*, edited by Susan Goodwin and Kate Huppatz, University of Sydney Press, 2010, pp. 175-193.

O'Reilly, Andrea. *Rocking the Cradle: Thoughts on Motherhood, Feminism and the Possibility of Empowered Mothering*. Demeter Press, 2006.

Ruddick, Sara. *Maternal Thinking: Toward a Politics of Peace*. 1989. Ballantine Books, 1990.

Mother India

SUBIMAL MISRA, TRANS. V. RAMASWAMY

And all realism itself
Has to be realized from imagination

Gorment

I lived in the Dum Dum airport. I've never seen my dad in my life, mother's simply Mother—what other name can a mother have? Yes, I had a brother. He was tiny, didn't get much to eat, fought with dogs for food from the waste pile. One day he was bitten on his face; his nose and face swelled up bad. He died after three days. My name's Malati. I've heard my father's name was Shambhu Mondal.

First put into Barrackpur sub-jail on 19 April 1974. Last April, she completed six years of life in jail. The registration no. is 7541 of 1974.

Malati does not know

Why

For the last six years

She lies

In prison

Without trial.

Here's the summary of the case as recorded in the court of the Sub-Divisional Judicial Magistrate of Barrackpur: On 2 April 1974, between 9:20 and 9:45 in the morning, the accused girl was seen eating from discarded packets lying on the floor of the lounge in Dum Dum airport, and consequently, she, Malati, was destroying the image of the Republic of India. Hence, Dum Dum police charged her under Section 290 of the Indian Penal Code and brought her to court for disposal of justice.

My mother worked in *babu* homes in the city. She left in the morning and only returned at night. She then made a few *rotis* and gave these to my brother and me to eat, with salt and chillies. On some days, she brought back rice and vegetables packed in a plate. We used to eat that. And the whole day I roamed the airport, searching for food. The police caught me one day. I destroyed the image of the great Indian nation. They took me to the police station. And then one day to the court. Eventually to jail.

It's there in the court papers. On 24 September 1974, in the court of the Barrackpur SDJM, after hearing everything, the order was passed that Malati be presented in court when instructed to do so by the court. Thereafter, for five years no one remembered her. Malati entered jail at the age of twelve. In the language of the court, she was an accused under trial. For five years, the honourable court completely effaced any memory of her.

Malati, too, gradually forgot everything. Whether in police lock-up or jail, at least one got something to eat there. She once said her mother's parental house was in Gomdipara, near Dum Dum. The police did not think it necessary to try to locate them. Malati said: mother, father or brother—I have nobody now. In the last six years, no one ever came to meet me, no one at all.

In the last year, she had to go to the Barrackpur court thirty times. The jail superintendent said: I came across the name out of the blue one day as I scanned through the register. Malati had not been brought to trial. She was rotting in jail without trial for five years. I immediately wrote a letter to the court. On receiving my letter, the judge himself wrote a letter to the state government. The judge's note remained stuck inside some file in the Writers' Building. Everybody forgot about Malati once again. I wrote once again to the judge. He wrote another letter to the government. May the honourable government be so kind as to arrange for the proper rehabilitation of this girl, in a proper environment. That order has so far crossed only three tables in the Writers' Building.

Malati wanted to learn some skill, tailoring or any kind of work, so that she could fend for herself. *Can't the gorment help me a little?* Yes, she knows the name of the prime minister of India. She had also heard that this was a great woman. Casting her eyes down to her toes, biting the nails of her left hand, she said: I really want to have a family, a handsome husband... I want to eat well twice a day—rice with sweet tamarind chutney.

Today, after such a long time, she does not remember that six years ago she had gone to forage for food thrown away by *babus* in the airport lounge, an offence for which six years of the child's life were lost in jail. In a jail in independent India. Without trial.

The Body

On Saturday morning, Tararani Bhuiyan, Manasi Dasi, Tarubala, and five children were killed while foraging coal from the garbage hillock in Dhapa. They were buried under a thirty-foot high heap of garbage. Like every day, on this day too at around nine in the morning, small children and womenfolk went to the garbage hillock on the Dhapa dumping ground to forage coal. The group dug a hole and burrowed their way in. Suddenly, there was a loud noise and the hillock of garbage collapsed. Only one woman, Angurbala Dasi, survived. Seven of those who died were from Pagladanga. Tararani alone was from Mathpukur.

One could see a bulldozer searching for the dead bodies under the thirty-foot high garbage hillock. Three or four squads of police had arrived; they had skillfully cordoned off the entire area. A few thousand people from the *bastis* of Mathpukur and the surrounding areas—emaciated, naked, half-naked, curious and agitated—stood outside the police cordon. The news reached the fire department around noon. They rushed to the accident site and using spades and hoes to move the earth, began the rescue work. But it wasn't possible to move a thirty-foot high hillock of earth using spades and hoes. The Municipal Corporation then phoned for a bulldozer to be sent from Palmer Bazar.

Now the corporation workers' eyes were on the jaws of the bulldozer. As it dug into the earth, tiny baskets emerged now and then. It was with just such baskets that early in the morning, a group of living humans dug a hole like rats and entered it to forage pieces of coal.

Suddenly, the public shouted aloud. A leg emerged from the earthen hillock and then disappeared. The bulldozer was then moved away, and they began digging the earth with spades. After about five minutes, the body of a girl of about twenty emerged, a crumpled lump wrapped in torn rags. The officers kept saying: There, we've found a body! The public raced toward the spot to identify the body.

On the other side, across the mud road, sitting beside another crumpled lump of a body wrapped in rags, was her father, an eighty-year-old man with shining white hair. The name of the body was Tarubala. Mother of five children. She had left in the morning, like every day, to forage coal. If they sold the coal, they would get about three rupees in the evening. She could feed her children. Someone said that Tarubala had told the daughter on her bosom that for the coming Puja, she would buy her a toy.

The girl now sat on a pile of dirt and put handfuls of earth into her mouth. Earth—yes, earth. With astonished eyes, she gazed fixedly at the crows flying around chaotically. All around her were many crows and a couple of sparrows. After searching continuously until eight in the evening, the fire brigade personnel and the officer-in-charge of Tiljala police station were drenched with perspiration: There are no more bodies buried under the earth. If there are, we'll look into that later. A police picket was posted in front of the garbage hillock.

The *basti* dwellers frequently came to the garbage hillock to forage coal. Someone said: they are prepared to take any kind of risk for just two handfuls of rice. This dangerous garbage hillock causes accidents, but it also provides a handful to eat once a day, said the white-haired eighty-year-old man, sitting beside his dead daughter's body. He knows that this kind of accident has occurred several times at the garbage hillock near Dunlop Bridge and that many people have died; everyone in the locality knew about it. He said: what will we people do—what will we eat? Would anyone willingly go to do such work, *babu*, only to die?

Patrimony

I see the boy returning everyday by the local train to Canning. A key—in lieu of the ritual piece of iron—hangs on his neck from a rag cord. He wears a half-*dhoti* made of a single cloth. A month's unwashed dirt on him. Dry hair that has never seen oil. Falling over the face. An earthen begging bowl in hand, some loose change in that. Seeing him, one would surmise from the ritual garb that his mother or father had died a few days ago. He goes around begging. Not ordinary begging, but for parental funerary duties. I see him every day. I've been seeing him for a year and a half.

—For how long is your parent mourning going on, boy? He didn't get alarmed, not the slightest bit.

—Tell me, what can I do, the *babus* don't want to give alms just like that. I thought about it a lot and chose this way. Please give me one of your cigarettes.

—You smoke?

—Why shouldn't I smoke? Can't we have tastes and desires?

—What do you do with the money, boy? Do you give it at home

or ... all these tastes and desires ...?

—Why won't I give it? ... My dad took another woman and went away. I live with Mother. With Mother and my small brother and sister.

—What does your mother do?

—Mother's not well now. She has a bad disease. She's in bed all day long. That's why I've chosen this line. When Mother was well, she used to come to sell toddy in the street in Calcutta.

—Do you too drink toddy?

—Yes, 'course I do, all of us drink. The youngest one, my brother, is eight months old now ... Mother has no milk ... so when he cries too much, Mother gives toddy to him too. He becomes calm when he drinks toddy. Why is drinking toddy bad, *babu*? So many sons of *bhadralok*, all of them gulp down glass after glass... Mother said all the *bhadralok* have only foul things in their mind.

—Your mother's illness?

—Do you want to know what the illness is, babu? It's a very shameful thing. Mother was returning home from Calcutta by the last train, after selling toddy. It was a night in the month of December. There was no one in the vendors' compartment that night. Finding an opportunity, two home guards and their pals all raped my mother that night. Mother told me everything; she wept her heart out on my shoulder. She told me a lot that day. She said it's the rule of the big folk. No one cares about the poor. The police and everyone else are there only for the suited-booted *bhadralok* and moneyed big folk. Give money and turn the case around. There's no one to protest. Let me grow up a bit, let me get strong... Mother's told me, it's I who have to take revenge.

Speaking from Beyond the Grave

Abjection and the Maternal Corpses of William Faulkner's *As I Lay Dying* and Suzan-Lori Parks's *Getting Mother's Body*

BIANCA BATTI

IN *THE MONSTROUS-FEMININE: Film, Feminism, Psychoanalysis,* Barbara Creed contends that all human societies have constructed ideas regarding "what it is about woman that is shocking, terrifying, horrific, abject" (1). As Creed points out, it would seem that such constructs often define woman's abjection through her sexuality and (bad) motherhood because "when woman is represented as monstrous it is almost always in relation to her mothering and reproductive functions" (7). Although Creed uses this discussion of gender to analyze film and the horror genre, her analysis of the manner in which women are abjected can, of course, be applied to other textual representations as well.

The idea of abjection seems especially helpful when considering the manner in which bad motherhood, sexuality, and female corporeality are represented in two specific texts, namely William Faulkner's *As I Lay Dying* and Suzan-Lori Parks's *Getting Mother's Body*. Significantly, both texts present two maternal corpses—those of Addie Bundren and Willa Mae Beede (respectively)—and these maternal corpses exemplify the concept of abjection in that they have been cast out of the symbolic order, which reveals, as Creed says, that the "ultimate in abjection is the corpse" (9). As such, Addie's and Willa Mae's deaths result in both women occupying a state of double abjection. Their maternal corpses, compounded by their already abject roles as sexual beings and bad mothers, render these women doubly cast out and marginalized.

I argue that Addie and Willa Mae's abject, maternal corpses challenge the social norms of the dominant patriarchal ideologies in which both women are entrenched. But both women encounter limitations, too, in their transgressive journeys—journeys on which they embark from beyond the grave. These transgressive journeys are ones that both Addie and Willa Mae begin in life, as well, through their positioning as bad, ambivalent, and sexual mothers. Thus, by unpacking these living and dead positionings, I hope to begin a conversation regarding how abjection can be a useful lens through which to consider the complex and often problematic ways motherhood and female sexuality are textually represented. Ultimately, the abject representations of Addie and Willa Mae hinge on their constructions as bad mothers.

The figure of the bad mother is repeatedly represented in texts throughout history. As Molly Ladd-Taylor and Lauri Umansky point out in the introduction to *Bad Mothers: The Politics of Blame in Twentieth-Century America*, "virtually every culture on historical record has had its wicked women, and in many cases their wickedness revolved around the reproductive function" (6). They go on to note that a "glance at the 'bad' mothers of any age reveals the fate of women who violated the gender norms of their time, whether by choice, by fiat, or by the force of circumstance" (6). Ladd-Taylor and Umansky explain the power structures in which women in the nineteenth century were located by highlighting the rigid definitions of "true womanhood" that begin to become apparent during this period: "Where previously womanhood was associated with sexuality, cunning, and immorality, the Victorian cult of 'true womanhood' defined women as pure, pious, domestic, and submissive. Their supposedly superior moral sensibility gave 'true' women dignity, increased their authority at home, justified their education, and defined their role in public life" (7). However, Ladd-Taylor and Umansky also note the precarious position that "true women," who were defined through their maternal roles, occupied: "Yet the sentimentalized Victorian mother perched on a shaky pedestal. The mother who lifted her voice too loudly or attended too diligently to her own needs felt the sting of familial, clerical, and community disapproval" (7). This precariously perched, maternally rendered "true" woman is also located within white "middle-class culture" (8).

Nineteenth-century renderings of good and bad motherhood

have extended into the ways we have come to think about motherhood in the twentieth and twenty-first centuries as well. Thus, even today, the "bad" mother comes to be defined in opposition to the true woman—the "good" mother—in that the bad mother is perceived as not selfless enough, not pure enough, not submissive enough, not domestic enough, not white enough, and not middle-class enough. The bad mother does not conform to the norms imposed upon women through the Victorian cult of "true womanhood"—norms that persist to this day. And I would argue that the bad mother's outright defiance of these norms reveals that the cult of true womanhood was a fallacy then and is a fallacy now, which is what makes the bad mother's transgressive nature so dangerous and subversive. It is the dangerous, subversive nature of the bad mother that often causes her to be marginalized and to be rendered abject.

In order to understand the abjected figure of the bad mother, it is necessary to define abjection a bit further. As Julia Kristeva explains, the abject is a representation of that which we fear and reject most; the abject is "that of being opposed to *I*" (230). This oppositionality not only defines the dominant ideology (by being the Other against which normativity is constructed) but also challenges this ideology at the same time: "From its place of banishment, the abject does not cease challenging its master ... it beseeches a discharge, a convulsion, a crying out" (230). The most exemplary abject figure is the corpse because the corpse "is cesspool, and death; it upsets even more violently the one who confronts it ... corpses *show me* what I permanently thrust aside in order to live" (231). Kristeva sees the corpse as "the ultimate in abjection," as Creed phrases it, because it is "death infecting life. Abject. It is something rejected from which one does not part, from which one does not protect oneself ... it beckons to us and ends up engulfing us" (232). This is why the abjection of the corpse is ontologically significant—it is an inherently ambiguous reminder of death in that we seek to cast it off and yet we cannot be rid of it; it is "death infecting life." As Kristeva points out, "It is thus not lack of cleanliness or health that causes abjection but what disturbs identity, system, order. What does not respect borders, positions, rules. The in-between, the ambiguous, the composite" (232).

Kristeva highlights the figure of the mother as a particularly abject one in her discussion of the "abject maternal." Sandra Chang-Kredl explains Kristeva's definition in terms of the generative power of the maternal body:

> Kristeva (1982) describes the underlying abject of the maternal as being her generative power. There is something about a potently creative woman that, in the unconscious landscape of the symbolic order, is feared as unnatural, dangerous and threatening ... This generative power must be subdued in order to maintain the illusion that the symbolic order is the only way to the creation of an individuated and fully constituted identity. The idea that a woman can have desires and, further, express these desires through creations, ideas, anger or leadership, is seen as unnatural and destructive. (356)

As Mary Caputi also explains, Kristeva finds the destructiveness of the abject maternal to be "inherently deconstructive" because motherhood "blurs the distinctions between self and other" by representing "'a permanent calling into question' of language, culture, and human subjectivity" (32). In other words, the maternal body is one that the child is connected to because it is the site of the child's creation, which results in the connection of the maternal to the construction of the self. Maura Sheehy notes the tension in this connection to the self because even though we are connected to the maternal body, "we all must abject our mothers to become subjects, to exist." She continues, "Haunted by our dependence, we abject her and at the social level anything we need to label 'foreign' so that we can continuously define and maintain our borders" (66). Yet these borders are difficult to maintain and define because of the manner in which our connection to the maternal body blurs and deconstructs such boundaries. As a result, the maternal body is abject because it both belongs and does not belong to the child. It is both a part of the child's subjectivity and counter to it. Thus, the blurring, deconstructing, questioning nature of the maternal—that is, the abject maternal—is subversive in its disturbing disruption of the boundaries of the self.

This disruption of boundaries is especially prevalent in the multiple manners in which the maternal bodies of Willa Mae and Addie are rendered abject and the multiple ways their abject maternal corpses trouble the boundaries of the self. In *As I Lay Dying*, Addie's abjection is represented, in part, through her sexuality. Addie says, "In the early spring it was worst. Sometimes I thought that I could not bear it, lying in bed at night" (Faulkner 162). Here, Addie acknowledges the fact that she is a sexual being, but she seems to view it in a negative way. It (her sexuality) is something that gets worse in the spring and is something she cannot bear. And because she cannot bear it, she marries Anse to satisfy her sexual need; however, she finds that she does not love Anse and because she feels betrayed by the concept of marital love, she begins an affair with Whitfield, a preacher: "While I waited for him in the woods, waiting for him before he saw me, I would think of him as dressed in sin. I would think of him as thinking of me as dressed also in sin ... I would think of the sin as garments which we would remove" (166). Addie's sexual agency goes against the social norms imposed upon the Southern women of her community. It is the sin in which she is dressed.

Her abjection is underscored by the fact that Addie is also a mother. In other words, Addie is both a sexual being and a maternal figure, a combination of traits that the patriarchal symbolic order typically rejects—a bad mother. Not only is Addie both sexual and a (bad) mother, she is a mother who despises her maternal role because, as Jill Bergman argues, "it is precisely motherhood that convinces Addie that living is terrible" (397). The birth of Cash, Addie's firstborn, makes her realize this: "And when I knew that I had Cash, I knew that living was terrible and that this was the answer to it" (163). Addie's abject position as a mother who rejects her maternal role—Addie's abject position as a bad mother—is highlighted when Cora Tull denounces her non-normative mothering: "Cora Tull would tell me I was not a true mother" (166). Since Addie is "not a true mother," since she is a bad mother who abhors her maternal role, she is rendered abject.

Addie's abjection is doubled upon her death, something for which she seems prepared: "I could just remember how my father used to say that the reason for living was to get ready to stay dead a long time" (161). Her abjection is underscored by the presence of her decayed corpse, a decay heralded, for instance, by the appearance of buzzards. As the character Armstid notes, "Along toward nine oclock it begun to get hot. That was when I see the first buzzard ... soon as I see them it was like I could smell it in the field a mile away from just watching them, and them circling and circling for everybody in the county to see what was in my barn" (177). Vardaman also invokes the smell of his mother's decayed flesh: "I can smell her ... can you smell her, too?" (206). Through these representations of the grotesque reality (and smell) of Addie's corpse, we are reminded of the abject nature of Addie's position in the symbolic order. Her corpse does not respect boundaries or rules; it forces all those who encounter it to smell and experience its decay. Her corpse signifies death infecting life, a disturbing of the social order. This abject disruption is layered on top of Addie's disruptive sexual agency and her rejection of maternal behaviour have already caused; in this way, we can think of Addie as doubly abjected.

The character of Willa Mae Beede in Suzan-Lori Parks's *Getting Mother's Body* allows us to conceive of this idea of the doubly abjected maternal corpse more fully, given that the novel is, in part, a response to *As I Lay Dying*. Laura Wright sheds light on the relationship between the two novels:

> In this novel, not only do Parks's characters dig up—literally "resurrecting"—the 'brownish-colored bones' of the dead blues singer Willa Mae Beede, but Parks herself plays the part of theatrical *sangoma* (a traditional African bone-casting healer) by digging into, translating, and adapting William Faulkner's *As I Lay Dying* (1930) to create a novel that resists a singular monologic narrative position ... Parks utilizes Faulkner's monologue-based style in a way that fosters intertextual dialogue. *Getting Mother's Body* signifies—in Henry Louis Gates Jr.'s sense—on Faulkner's text to create what Parks describes as "a novel in voices" about race and women. In so doing she provides an African American counterpart that speaks to, honors, and borrows from Faulkner's work. (141)

As a result of the manner in which Parks extends the conversation that Faulkner's work began, her work effectively "stages an overt performance of gendered identity that extends Faulkner's work beyond the realm of white, heterosexual identification" (Wright 141).

This extension is achieved partly through the representation of Willa Mae's abjection in *Getting Mother's Body*, a representation that begins in a similar manner to Addie's. For instance, like Addie, Willa Mae's sexuality is highlighted throughout the novel. For instance, Willa Mae is often referred to as being "fast;" Dill, Willa Mae's lover, states, "She was fast as this truck. Hell, she was faster than this truck, she was fast as lightning" (Parks 140). And also like Addie, Willa Mae seeks to distance herself from normative maternal behaviour, as represented by her rejection of the title "mother." As her daughter Billy explains, "She liked being called her name ... I callt her 'Mother' in my head, but not out loud ... That was the way she wanted it" (173). Willa Mae's rejection of motherhood is also apparent in her fatal attempt to abort her second child. The ideas of birth and death often occur concurrently within the figure of Willa Mae. Her desire to terminate her second pregnancy ultimately results in her own death. Also, it seems interesting that when "Willa was pregnant with Billy, Willa had a taste for dirt" (223). The dirt, here, brings to mind the idea of the grave. The ambiguous conflation of life and death is exactly what renders Willa Mae a (doubly) abject figure. Yet although Addie's death and her corpse are portrayed in grotesque ways, Willa Mae's death is revealed to us differently. Indeed, we do not encounter many images of Willa Mae's decaying dead body; instead, Willa Mae portrays her own grave to us through one of her blues songs: "Deep down in this hole / It's a cold cold lonesome hole / I made my bed / Now I'm laying in it all alone" (218). In this way, Willa Mae's voice continues from beyond the grave.

And this is where the subversive and transgressive potential of these two abject figures emerges. Both Addie and Willa Mae assert their voices from beyond the grave. Whereas Willa Mae speaks through song, Addie speaks with the decayed flesh of her body. Addie's corpse cries for revenge; she explains, "my revenge would be that [Anse] would never know I was taking revenge. And

when Darl was born I asked Anse to promise to take me back to
Jefferson when I died" (Faulkner 165). Thus, although, as Cora
Tull says, Addie's death means that "she has her reward in being
free of Anse Bundren" (86), it also means that she can make her
abjection known and forces Anse to share her abject state by
making him take her decaying corpse to Jefferson. She also forces
all those who encounter her body on this journey to experience
her abjection; therefore, Addie's corpse forces her community to
confront not only their own anxieties regarding death but also the
various hardships forced onto women. As Cora Tull says, "It's a
hard life on women, for a fact" (29).

In this context, we begin to view the abject Addie as a representation of what Kristeva calls "the deject": "A deviser of territories,
languages, works, the *deject* never stops demarcating his universe
whose fluid confines … constantly question his solidity and impel
him to start afresh. A tireless builder, the deject is in short a *stray*.
He is on a journey… And the more he strays, the more he is saved"
(235). The deject embarks on a straying journey to question the
boundaries of the universe, the social order in which she is located. Addie embarks on such a straying through the journey of
her corpse across the South. This straying journey allows her to
challenge the boundaries and restrictions that have been placed on
women through binaristic definitions of normality; in short, Addie's
journey forces people to confront the multi-leveled manifestations
of abjection exemplified by her corpse.

The transgressive nature of Willa Mae's corpse, though, functions a bit differently. Whereas the journey of Addie's corpse is
motivated by spite and vengeance, Willa Mae's influence from beyond the grave allows for more positive emotional undertones—a
reimagining of familial configurations. In other words, the Beedes'
journey to get mother's body (as opposed to the Bundrens' journey
to get rid of mother's body) allows for the growing of familial ties
among the group because they come together to help Billy. The
abject nature of Willa Mae's corpse helps them to establish this
connectivity, as seen when Teddy remarks that "Willa Mae ended
up in the ground," to which Dill responds, "We all end up in the
ground" (Parks 36). Willa Mae's abject corpse requires her family
and friends to confront the idea of their own deaths, but in a way

that ties them together and establishes communal bonds. As Billy says, "When I seen her bones I knew what we all knew, that we's all gonna end up in a grave someday, but there's stops in between there and now" (258). And it is the "between there and now" that affords more potential for the establishment of deeper familial connectivity for the Beedes.

Indeed, as Billy notes, "Willa Mae had her own way of doing everything" (183). Just as Willa Mae "had her own way" of doing things, so too, now, do all the Beedes. They have their own way of (re)defining family and community, one that goes against normative nuclear constructions. In this way, we can view *Getting Mother's Body* as a text "that foreground[s] the black family and celebrate[s] its non-nuclear nature"—a function of African American literature that as Venetria K. Patton explains, explores the living role of the ancestor (8). We can, then, see Billy as being "in need of ancestral cultural healing in order to achieve well-being to tap into ancestral knowledge and strength" (15). As such, Willa Mae is the ancestor who "must reach beyond the grave" to guide her daughter, her family, and her community (16).

Patricia Hill Collins also touches the role of community in fostering youth in *Black Feminist Thought*. In her discussion of the collective nature of motherhood in many African American communities, Hill Collins explains the role of "othermothers" in this network of motherhood:

In many African-American communities, fluid and changing boundaries often distinguish biological mothers from other women who care for children. Biological mothers, or bloodmothers, are expected to care for their children. But African and African-American communities have also recognized that vesting one person with full responsibility for mothering a child may not be wise or possible. As a result, othermothers—women who assist bloodmothers by sharing mothering responsibilities—traditionally have been central to the institution of Black motherhood. (178)

This network of bloodmothers and othermothers is significant because as Hill Collins contends, it "illustrates how African-influenced understandings of family have been continually reworked to help African-Americans as a collectivity cope with and resist oppression. Moreover, these understandings of woman-centered kin networks become critical in understanding broader African-American understandings of community" (183). These woman-centred kin networks grow among the characters of *Getting Mother's Body* as the events of the novel unfold. And the growth of this collective network is fostered, in part, by the path the characters take to get Willa Mae's body.

But there are limits to the abject potentiality of these two corpses. Addie and Willa Mae both must die to challenge the social order, and death, obviously, is not the ideal way to achieve such ends. As Billy says, "I'd rather show up in a bus than in a hearse" (Parks 50). Thus, it would seem that both texts find it difficult to conceive of possibilities for women other than death or conformity. Jill Bergman posits that Faulkner sees Addie's sexuality and motherhood as incommensurable, which results in the fact that Addie "dies, suggesting that 'this' answer to the terrible life of a rural Southern woman can only be death" (406). Therefore, in *As I Lay Dying*, the implication seems to be that "while life is hard for women, that's just how life is" (Bergman 401). Women must either conform to this life or die in any attempt to challenge it. Willa Mae, too, ultimately undoes herself in her desire not to be a mother because she dies in her attempts to terminate her pregnancy. Billy, on the other hand, decides not to terminate her pregnancy—a decision that reveals that death or motherhood is the only choice afforded to women in this text. Nothing else is made available or possible for them.

In death, both Willa Mae and Addie experience an inversion. Addie's body, for instance, is inverted in her coffin: "They had laid her in it reversed ... they had laid her in it head to foot" (Faulkner 82). And as Dill explains to Teddy, Willa Mae's headstone is inverted at her gravesite: "She tells me the headstone's at the wrong end but she didn't lay it" (Parks 235). Although Addie forces people to confront her abject position, her body is, nonetheless, constrained by the coffin, and her sexuality is constrained by the social order; she cannot get past the constraints of her (decayed) flesh. Willa Mae, though, experiences a different inversion. Her body is not inverted in the grave; rather, her headstone is. The headstone, then, becomes a space of discourse, one that announces the identity of the deceased. Because of this, Willa Mae's inversion is not one of the body (like Addie) but one of the voice. Willa Mae uses her ancestral voice to help her daughter establish a non-normative configuration of community and family. Therefore, Willa Mae is not simply a decayed corpse crying for revenge. Rather, she is the ancestral living dead who lives on in the memory of her community. This role is especially represented through Willa Mae's blues songs: "Hey everybody, wontcha gather round / Roll up yr sidewalks / Lay yr red carpet down / Cause I'm here. / This gal is here" (90). Indeed, although she is dead, Willa Mae is here and lives on in the memory of those who knew her.

But there are limitations, too, in the positive potential in Willa Mae's ancestral motherhood and the manner in which her motherhood sheds light on the complicated nature of motherhood for black women. Hill Collins highlights this complicated nature in her discussion of the manner in which black motherhood is often represented:

> Within African-American communities, women's innovative and practical approaches to mothering under oppressive conditions often bring recognition and foster their empowerment. But this situation should not obscure the costs of motherhood to many U.S. Black women. Black motherhood is a fundamentally contradictory institution. African-American communities value motherhood, but Black mothers' ability to cope with intersecting oppressions of race, class, gender, sexuality, and nation should not be confused with transcending the injustices characterizing these oppressions. Black motherhood can be rewarding, but it can also extract high personal costs. The range of Black women's reactions to motherhood and the ambivalence that many Black women feel about mothering reflect motherhood's contradictory nature. (195)

Thus, although Willa Mae's ancestral voice is an empowered and empowering one, black motherhood as "a fundamentally contradictory institution" is also represented through the figure of Willa Mae. Even though in death Willa Mae may be an empowered ancestral figure for her daughter and her community, in life she was, contradictorily, a mother who was inherently ambivalent regarding her maternal role. As a result of both of these characterizations (Willa Mae as empowered ancestor and Willa Mae as ambivalent mother), Willa Mae occupies a liminal space; she is good and bad, supportive and absent, and powerful and abject. The fact that she is all these things troubles the boundaries of normative categorizations for identity construction. As such, Willa Mae textually represents Hill Collins's examination of black motherhood as a contradictory and complicated institution—a space similar to that of Kristeva's space of abjection and the manner in which the abject troubles the boundaries of normative social structures and constructions of self.

It is through these different manifestations of abjection represented by the bodies of Addie and Willa Mae that we understand the challenges women face in living outside the norms of the social order. These are the gendered challenges that Jane M. Ussher explores in *Managing the Monstrous Feminine*. She argues that although the abject "stands for that which we most dread ... the hidden, unacknowledged, and feared parts of identity and society ... the 'other' against which normality is defined" (6), these manifestations are often rendered in gendered ways. But she also stresses that "this is not to say that the female body *is* abject or polluted, it has merely been positioned as such, with significant implications for women's experiences of inhabiting a body so defined" (7). This is also not to say that abject women—like Willa Mae and Addie—are necessarily always positioned "as inevitably subjugated" because of their cast-off state of being (18); rather, both Addie and Willa Mae work to challenge their subjugated positions and transgress boundaries from beyond the grave. Therefore, the seemingly pathological deviance of abjection is not as inevitable as it may seem because abjection is ambivalent, disruptive, and potentially transgressive.

By examining the manner in which these two texts make use of representations of the idea of abjection, we can begin a conversation about both the nuanced meanings made in these texts as well as the manner in which the body functions in making such meanings. Such meanings, as the conversation between Faulkner's and Parks's novels reveals, complicate our understanding of the ways the meaning made through the body can be constructed on the basis of gender and race. Such meanings also complicate our understanding of the ways bodies can trouble these raced and gendered boundaries through the disruptive and transgressive positioning of abject maternal embodiment. For, as Kristeva says, "Significance is indeed inherent in the human body" (237).

WORKS CITED

Bergman, Jill. "'this was the answer to it': Sexuality and Maternity in *As I Lay Dying*." *Mississippi Quarterly*, vol. 49, no. 3, 1996, pp. 393-407.

Caputi, Mary. "The Abject Maternal: Kristeva's Theoretical Consistency." *Women and Language*, vol. 16, no. 2, 1993, pp. 32-37.

Chang-Kredl, Sandra. "Coraline's Split Mothers: The Maternal Abject and the Childcare Educator." *Continuum*, vol. 29, no. 3, 2015, pp. 354-64.

Creed, Barbara. *The Monstrous-Feminine: Film, Feminism, Psychoanalysis*. Routledge, 1993.

Faulkner, William. *As I Lay Dying*. Random House, 1964.

Hill Collins, Patricia. *Black Feminist Thought: Knowledge, Consciousness, and the Politics of Empowerment*. Routledge, 2000.

Kristeva, Julia. "Approaching Abjection." *The Portable Kristeva*, edited by Kelly Oliver, Columbia University Press, 1997, pp. 229-47.

Ladd-Taylor, Molly, and Lauri Umansky. "Introduction." *"Bad" Mothers: The Politics of Blame in Twentieth-Century America*, edited by Molly Ladd-Taylor and Lauri Umansky, New York University Press, 1998, pp. 1-28.

Parks, Suzan-Lori. *Getting Mother's Body: A Novel*. Random House, 2003.

Patton, Venetria K. *The Grasp That Reaches Beyond the Grave: The Ancestral Call in Black Women's Texts*. State University of New York Press, 2013.

Sheehy, Maura. "Sparring with the Eternal Maternal Abject."

Studies in Gender and Sexuality vol. 13, no. 1, 2012, pp. 65-7.

Ussher, Jane M. *Managing the Monstrous Feminine: Regulating the Reproductive Body*. Routledge, 2006.

Wright, Laura. "Casting the Bones of Willa Mae Beede: Passing and Performativity in Suzan-Lori Parks's *Getting Mother's Body*." *Tulsa Studies in Women's Literature*, vol. 30, no. 1, 2011, pp. 141-57.

Blue Robe

BERNADETTE WAGNER

B Y CHANCE, I CAUGHT Mom's tears that October afternoon, two days after my parents' nineteenth wedding anniversary dinner at our new house in the city. They'd determined it best for the family to relocate from the farm to "try again" after Mom's affair with her boss came to light. I had already been living in the city since graduation, working a summer job with the provincial civil service. I'd started my first semester of university in September and moved to our new home after my summer savings ran out at the end of September.

Dinner was a disaster. Tension, all that was unsaid around me, churned my stomach. Anger rocketed with every mastication. A farce, I thought. They're engaging my three younger siblings—and me—in a farce. Why are they pretending? I stared at the ugly wallpaper on the dining room wall, its curved velvety black patterns against a red background reminding me of a hotel scene in some old movie. I could not continue playing along. My chair slid back on the plush brown carpet when I pushed away from the table. Dishes and cutlery rattled. Glances from Mom and my sisters. My brother continued shovelling mashed potatoes and gravy into his mouth. I couldn't look at Dad. I stood to my full height.

"This is bullshit," I said in the most calm, cool, and collected voice I could muster. It got everyone's attention. All my siblings looked up at me, darted quick glances at each other, at my parents, then pretended to carry on with their meal, dipping pieces of beef into pools of gravy or moving peas and carrots around on the plate. No one said a word. I didn't look at my parents, didn't care what anyone thought, and I didn't stick around. I stomped to my basement bedroom, my tears a trailer for the sobs that were to come. Deep inside, I knew that even more sadness and grief were to come. I've always had those feelings of knowingness. But I hoped that for once I'd be wrong.

If anyone had come to console me that evening, I don't recall it. Giving comfort and solace is not a typical response to emotional outbursts, not in my family of origin anyway. It's part of being a good German Lutheran, or so I'd learned, where expressions of emotion are inappropriate, excessive. They might bring attention on you. What would the neighbours think? Although I do try to avoid it now, I am still perfectly capable, almost forty years later, of bottling emotion until it explodes all over the room.

I called a friend after I'd recovered enough from dinner to speak. I drove my little Vauxhaul to her nearby apartment where she and her boyfriend were having a beer. He was a year older than us and able to legally purchase alcohol. We decided to watch a movie, smoke dope, and drink our beer. As one of the stupid youth brigade of the early 1980s, I drove myself home after midnight, when I knew everyone would be in bed, then left for my 8:30 class without speaking to a member of my family.

Two days after the anniversary dinner, I cut classes early. I'd injured my leg and scheduled a doctor's appointment for the afternoon. With extra time beforehand, I stopped in at home and discovered my mother emptying dresser drawers, closet shelves, the top of the chiffoniere, packing nineteen years of marriage into a couple of old suitcases and a few cardboard boxes. I was not surprised at her leaving. I knew this was coming. And I knew she believed she had a chance at some kind of dream love. What shocked me, even at eighteen years of age, was that she'd leave without a word to her children. I don't recall what words I bellowed at her, but I bellowed. All I remember hearing was her voice, almost shouting through her sobs, "I know you're going to hate me for this!"

My body quivered. I turned my back on her, walked down to my room and cried again. Then I washed my red eyes with cool water, quickly applied new mascara, and left, again without a word. By the time I got home, she had driven off into her dream. That she left before 3:30, before the end of the school day, before my younger sisters came home from school, suggested to me a lack of courage.

I visited the same friend that night, same routine. Got stoned, got drunk, drove home. It would be a pattern for several years, with various friends. By the end of that October, I'd left university for a blue velour robe that I'd step into and zip up each morning, wear all day while I cooked full meals for a family of five, managed groceries and household supplies, kept the kitchen sparkling clean, helped my sisters with homework, drove them to piano and skating lessons, braided their hair for class photos, and tended to extended family events such as birthdays and anniversaries.

The role was easy to slip into, something I had familiarity with. I had time and no inclination to occupy myself with much other than watching soap operas and movies. *Ordinary People* became a much loved favourite. *On Golden Pond*, too. But nothing comforted me more than that soft, deep azure blue robe I wore daily, until the zipper broke and the seat shone like the stove I polished each Saturday.

Mother-Witch and Other Poems

COURTNEY BATES-HARDY

Sometimes I hate them: my children
and their chirping open mouths. I want
to lead them from the page and back
to the woods they came from.

But I know they will toddle back,
a trail of crumbs in their wake,
and I will lift their fragile bones to my lap,
knowing each ribbed stanza against my fingertips.

The truth is that I starve
                without them.

I must press my lips to their budding mouths
and let my chewed bread fall

to their trembling tongues;
I must fatten them on the page,

until they leave me,
burning in my empty oven.

"I Understand You, Stepmother" (from *House of Mystery*, 2016)

I understand you, stepmother,

scrutinizing your pores in the glass,
magnified every year
where dirt gathers just beneath
the reach of your ragged fingernails.

You've driven out the blemish
with blood; when it scars,
you dig again.

Your skin covers a death's head:
those generations before.

You memorize your mothers' lines,
the creases from their eyes
and down their cheeks.

Do they still see their former faces?
Your mother's anorexia
pervades your bone-fear,
your grandmother's breasts
are hollow caves after cancer,
while yours swell when you press
your nipples into a fairy ring:
if you go in,
you'll never come back.

Your mother's madness
made her calm
but you are red and raging.

You know your children will carry
the mark of blood on their foreheads.

And when they look in the mirror,
they'll decide
which mother to keep
and which to smash.

"Grandmother" (from *House of Mystery*, 2016)

She is young and cold;
the long lines of her body
angling into the white sky:
a stark tree in a field
of curving drifts and crisp
snowflake lashes.

She is a frozen wave,
believing nothing
could be other than what it is
now: pristine and sharp
as inhaling ice.

She grows old in a season,
rounding out like the sky,
suffusing icy angles:
light drips down.

Her skin is latticed,
and blue tinges the
edges of her eyes,
like a bud on a branch.

She knows everything
will end, even her.

She is a crashing wave,
a snow drift dissolved overnight;
we awake to a lawn of water
stretching out before us,
blinking her blue, blue eyes.

Her cheek is soft and wrinkled,
tissue thin.

Eclipse (from *House of Mystery*, 2016)
(*after George MacDonald's "Little Daylight"*)

My mother cursed her body
as I was born and so I reflect
her moonlit figure
as it burns away.

I remember her emptiness
before I was born.

We waxed and waned with the moon
that shone through the trees,
paralleled prison dream.

When I swell,
I pull at my clothes,
the choke of my jeans
that grate against bones.

The lines on my waist
mimic craters on the moon:
dark circles on pale skin.

When I shrink,
I delight in my loss,
my black shirt floats
around a white belly.

I wait
for a moment
I do not recognize:
the moon absorbs the sun.

If I go too far,
I slowly age,
a drooping branch,
curving around the sky,
a brittle leaf falls.

Notes from Tinkle

MADHULIKA LIDDLE

THE LETTER WAS WRITTEN in Hindi, the words misspelled and the letters shaky. The page was from a school notebook, cheap and thin, its lines in groups of four. The type used to teach cursive writing.

"Who brought this?" I asked, as I heaved the bag of vegetables onto the kitchen counter. Amma was stirring the *dal*, her grey hair standing out all about her head, escaping the meagre bun perched on her nape.

"I don't know," she said. "I found it tucked into the grill of the window." She did not have to say which window; between the two tiny rooms that make up our home, there is only one window. "What does it say?"

I read it out to her. *Ma. I want to see you. When will you come and get me? I love you so much. Tinkle.*

"'Tinkle?'" Amma said, moving the *dal* off the burner and putting on a frying pan, pouring in mustard oil. "Who is that?"

I shrugged. I was too weary to think. Too drained. "It must be some child's school essay."

Amma nodded. I could see she wasn't convinced. I could not be bothered, I thought, in a burst of irritation.

The next moment, I felt guilty. I owed Amma my sanity. Papa's death in a car accident when I was just ten years old had sent my depression-prone mother over the brink, and it had fallen on Amma—my mother's old *ayah*, who had come to stay with us after Papa's death—to take over. Amma had nobody of her own, and we needed someone, if only to be a shoulder to cry on.

Amma proved to be much more. She was a far better house-keeper than Ma, and at a time when Papa's pension was proving woefully inadequate, she kept our home on an even keel, running along smoothly. Or as smoothly as it could, given Ma's frequent mood swings: the sudden sunniness, which would send her rushing off to Wenger's to buy pastries, and the just as sudden bouts of depression, which would make her talk of committing suicide.

And one day she did. Amma was with me, accompanying me home from the bus stop where my school bus dropped me off. We entered the house to find Ma hanging, her sturdy red *khadi dupatta* wound around her neck. Her eyes bulged, her face was swollen, purple. Amma was the one who cut her down, who called the neighbours. Who did everything.

"Essays are not that short, are they?" Amma said, as she added a spoonful of mustard seeds to the oil and stood back, waiting for them to stop spluttering. They spat all across the stainless steel top of the stove, leaving droplets of oil and exploded seeds. "When you used to go to school, your essays were always long. Always at least a page." She tilted in cubed peeled potatoes, and stirred briskly.

"What happened today, then?" she asked, her voice neutral, as if this wasn't the one thing that she had been wanting to know ever since I had stepped into the house.

"The next hearing is fixed for April. The twenty-first."

"Oh. But hadn't the lawyer said...?" Her voice trailed off.

"They say a lot of things, Amma. She was probably just trying to keep my spirits up. Now it looks as if it will go on a while longer."

I did not tell Amma about Prachi, whom I always ran into at the coffee machine in the office. She had discovered about my protracted divorce and had shared her own story. Ten years, she said, and in the course of it, her ex-husband's lawyer had retired and passed the case to his junior. Such a shambles, what with the house and the property and the bank accounts. "No children, thank God," she had said, sipping from the paper cup. "In that sense, I had an advantage over you."

And though I did not mention it to Prachi, she had had other advantages. One, that she was well off, having inherited a flat, a cottage in Kasauli, a well-filled bank account and sundry other odds and ends from wealthy parents. The other, which stemmed from her lack of financial difficulties, was the fact that she could afford the best divorce lawyer in Delhi. Mine was the best I could afford after I had paid for the basic necessities for Amma and me. Rent, food, electricity, water, transport. We had not seen a movie in ages. The last time I remembered eating out was when we stopped for *chaat* at a roadside stall.

The inexperience, the relative mediocrity, of my lawyer was now beginning to show itself.

"Well," said Amma with a sigh of resignation as she chopped spinach, the red plastic handle of the little vegetable knife tucked firmly into her curled fist. Broad leaves, glossy from water, going in under the gleaming blade, coming out from under Amma's fingers shredded into thin green ribbons. "As long as she is able to get you alimony." She winced, and for a moment, I thought she had cut herself. It was a stupid thought because Amma, when it comes to cooking, is like an automaton. So quick, the eye cannot see. So brave, so sure, so precise.

She was not hurt. She only looked up at me, guilt in her eyes, briefly before she turned her attention back to the spinach. "No," she corrected herself. "Not alimony. That is not important. Abhay."

Yes, I nodded. We knew that, both of us. Even Sudhir, my husband who was not yet officially ex, knew that. That it was not the alimony that mattered, but my son, ten years old and the only reason I had hung onto Sudhir for so long. Two years earlier, when Sudhir and I were still living in the same house, I used to tolerate his constant neglect—and the abuse, the only time he eased up on that neglect—because of Abhay. Because I knew I could not live without my child. The child who had lived under my heart for nine months and in my heart from the moment I had known of his existence.

I had wept, pleaded with Sudhir, telling him I would do whatever he wished, if only he would let me stay on. It embarrassed me to think of that now; how low could I have stooped? How could I have gone down on my knees before a man like that, and begged him, told him I'd take anything he meted out to me, if only he'd not separate me from Abhay? It was little consolation that when Sudhir literally picked me up and threw me out, I didn't try to sneak back in.

But Abhay. Oh, it still hurt to think of him. I could not remember, even, the last time I had seen him. In those early days, I thought. Perhaps one of those frantic times when I hung about outside his school, peering in and trying to catch a glimpse of him between the time he emerged from the gate and walked to the bus. Or was it later, hovering furtively outside what had once been my home, on a weekend, hoping to see Abhay go to the park for his evening game of football with the neighbourhood boys?

Sudhir had stopped sending Abhay to school in the bus. The driver had been deputed to ferry him, and the school had been informed that Abhay's mother was no longer allowed to meet him. And Sudhir himself had begun escorting Abhay to the park in the evening.

And the police, when I had gone to them, could do little. The bored-looking inspector who had listened to my complaint had interrupted me even before I was halfway through what I wanted to say, and had held up a hand.

"Madam," he had said, "This is your domestic affair. The police have more important things to do than sort out quarrels between husbands and wives."

It was true, I thought in a later, saner, moment. Sudhir had broken no law.

"It can take long," Prachi had said, speaking with the wisdom of bitter experience. "More so because it's not an amicable parting of ways. That's what they say, no? An amicable parting of ways."

She had smiled, her perfectly shaped lips curving up at the corners in a sardonic smile.

"As if it really could be ever *completely* amicable. If you don't like him enough to stay married to him, it means he disappointed you, no? And disappointment always leaves a bitter taste in the mouth."

Oh, it did. Very bitter. And that was one reason I could not let Abhay stay on with Sudhir. Because Sudhir, I knew, would fill his mind with all the rancour that Sudhir himself felt for me. Every day I spent away from Abhay, I wondered: would I ever really get my son back? Even if the law handed him back to me, would I get back Abhay as I had known him—sweet, loving, *my* son—or would I get a younger version of Sudhir?

I made coffee for myself. "Amma," I said, pouring it into the mug. "The lawyer says it doesn't look as if the judge will let me have Abhay. She said I should be prepared for that."

Amma's hands stilled. For once, her composure abandoned her. She put down the knife, wiped her hands on the end of her crumpled purple-and-beige cotton *sari*, and sat down on the little cane stool in the corner. For a few minutes, she sat there, her fingers wringing the end of her *sari*, her gaze flitting from me to her lap, to the window. Everywhere and nowhere.

"But Abhay is your son," she said, her voice choked. "I thought they always gave the child to the mother to bring up. Don't they? The child's place is with the mother. That was what I had always heard. Isn't that true? Won't they do that?" As if saying it over and over again would make it come true. I wished that were possible.

I went to lean against the window, looking out. This had been, to some extent, my reaction too when my lawyer had broken the news to me. This denial, this frantic questioning. And I had been given the answer to that. The answer that I now passed on.

"Not necessarily, Amma," I replied. "They also look at the parents' capability, their finances, the child's age, things like that. My financial condition is"—I swallowed a sip of coffee— "fragile." It would be even more fragile by the time the divorce was through, and everybody knew it. The judge included.

"Just because your husband has money, they will give Abhay to him? That is unfair."

I did not say anything. What was there to say?

"What is it?" I heard Amma say.

"Hmm?"

"You're frowning. What is it?"

Laughter, bitter acrid laughter bubbled up within me. As if I had no cause to frown. I shook my head, tamping down my sarcasm.

"There's someone outside the railing," I remarked. "A little girl."

I could see her clearly from where I stood beside the window, although I doubted she would be able to see me, even if she looked up. And she was not looking up. A small girl, wearing a school uniform that was faded from countless washes. She was sitting on a fallen block of concrete—once a base for a telephone pole—that lay next to our fence. Leaning down, hunched over something in her lap.

A stray from the municipal school at the end of the road, I thought. Stopping for a breather on her way home. To admire a ladybird, a pretty wildflower? The thought made me smile, then, at my own naïveté. Did little girls still gush over the things I had found so fascinating when I was small? Did they still have the time to notice ladybirds and daisies and the glossy black beads on lantana bushes?

I was turning away, off to rinse out my now-empty coffee mug, when I saw something that made me stop. The girl had stood up and was reaching into the shabby school bag slung from her shoulders. Pushing in what looked, at this distance, like a notebook. Then, without a moment's hesitation, she walked right up to our gate. I saw her stop there, in front of it. She paused and reached out. There was something white in her hand: a sheet of paper, folded, I thought. As if she were about to impale it on one of the spikes that rose above the battered body of the gate.

Then, as if she thought better of it, she turned and went away.

Amma had gone back to her cooking, so I said nothing to her. There were many other worries in life; a strange little girl who had paused briefly and inexplicably outside our house was hardly something to fret about.

And then, three days later, when I came home from work, Amma handed me a note. "It was wedged into the gate," she said. Terse, quiet.

"What happened? Why are you looking so gloomy, Amma?"

"Read the note, Manjiri."

Ma. Sudha said that you have gone away. She said she heard Chachi telling her sister. You will be back won't you, Ma? I think of you all the time. When will you come? Tinkle.

I read it through, then again.

"I wonder where she went," Amma said, breaking in, holding out a glass of water. I took it from her and drank it down. It was cold, the stainless steel of the glass already dewy on the outside. But it did nothing to dissolve the lump in my throat.

"Perhaps she just went away on work," I suggested. It sounded lame, even to my own ears. "Perhaps she needed to go to another town. To look after a relative, to attend to business. Something."

"A child old enough to write that is not so young that she could not have been told," Amma said, her tone sombre. "She is old enough to understand if her mother had a genuine reason to go."

"We don't know, Amma," I said, wearily. "It could be anything. It could be the ravings of a child who hates her real mother and has concocted a dream mother whom she would rather exchange for her own."

Amma looked at me as if I had gone mad. I thought I had, too.

But she said nothing then. We went about our work, she preparing dinner, me making a cup of coffee before I got down to attending to the laundry, folding, ironing. I was in the middle of ironing a *salwar-kurta* for the next day when a shadow fell across the ironing board. "You know it's nothing of the sort," Amma said. "That child's mother is gone. And she misses her."

I carried on, straightening out a sleeve, pressing in neat straight lines, curving in at the armhole seam.

"We should find out."

"How, Amma? Wait outside the gate and grab her the next time she comes around? Ask her—what? 'What happened to your mother, Tinkle? When did she disappear? How long has she been gone? Tell us; we're burning up with curiosity.' Is that what we should say?"

There was deep pain in Amma's eyes. I felt awful. I had felt awful even as I had said those words, but I had gone on, unable to stop. You know how it is when you are close to someone, when you think of them as an extension of yourself. When you know them so well and they know you so well that you hardly stop to think of them as different from yourself. You pull down barriers. You become more loving. And, sometimes, more angry, more rude, more reckless with your emotions.

"I'm sorry, Amma," I said. "I did not mean to be rude. I'll see what I can do."

It took another glimpse of the girl—Tinkle, I should call her, I knew her name by now—and another note from her before I decided to do something about it. Perhaps it was the note, the sad little letter with its words partially obscured by splotches of moisture.

Ma, did you go away because I was very naughty? Kamla didi tells me I am naughty, that she doesn't want me around. I'm sorry. Ma, please come back, please. I won't be naughty any more. I am trying.

It was Sunday. I was in, so I saw Tinkle, saw her put the note between two of the spikes on our gate. Amma was out, gone for her weekly stroll through the park, followed by two hours of sitting on a bench and watching the world go by: it was her way of gathering strength for the week to come. When she came back just before sunset, I did not tell her about Tinkle or the latest note.

Instead, the next morning, as I shut the gate behind me, I took out my phone and called the office to say I might be a little late. Half an hour, no more.

The local municipal school was a five minute walk from home. Small, dingy classrooms, a bare playground with a row of short *karanj* trees along one wall to provide some shade and the principal's office near the gate. The chatter of childish voices filled the air, some drifting out from classrooms, others—louder, more exuberant—coming from the playground, where about thirty children played. Boys kicking around a battered football, girls playing hopscotch. A woman teacher in a *salwar kurta*, her *dupatta* wrapped securely about an ample waist, sat on a bench under a tree and watched them with a bored look on her face.

"That must be Tinkle from the *basti*," said the principal. She was a thin little woman with close-cropped grey hair, her spectacles hanging on her chest from a black chain slung about her neck. She had polished them and put them on to see the file that the secretary had brought her after much rummaging about among the school records, and now she closed the file and sat back. "You know the *basti*? The slum down the road?"

Yes, I did. It was at the far end of the road, a ten-minute walk from our home.

"Who are her guardians?" I asked. Perhaps I could go and meet them, find out more. Where was her mother, who was she, where had she gone. If she was only gone, not dead as I feared she was.

The principal pulled her spectacles back onto the bridge of her nose and peered at the file. "Ah," she said. "Ah. She stays in foster care, but her guardian is listed as a woman from an NGO." She told me the name of the NGO, of the woman who was named as Tinkle's guardian, and of the woman whose address was written down in the file as being Tinkle's home. She did not know if the girl had been orphaned or abandoned or whether the woman she stayed with was a relative or not.

I stepped out of the principal's cool, curtained room and out into the sunlight. It was well past ten; by the time I got to office, I would have to apply for a half day's leave, even though I'd have been late by only two hours. I could do that, forget about Tinkle and her past. And her future. Forget about whether she had any living relatives and whether the woman she stayed with treated her well or not.

I would not be able to forget. I rummaged about in my bag and pulled out the diary in which I had scribbled down the name and address of the woman from the NGO.

Firoza was a young woman in her early twenties, in jeans and a purple *kurti*. She was bright and enthusiastic but did not know much about Tinkle beyond what I had already learned at the school. She was eight years old, an average student, rather shy and withdrawn. "I don't think the woman she lives with is any relative," Firoza admitted sheepishly. She must have noticed the blankness in my expression. She added, "I'm sorry I can't be of more help. I'm new here, you see; Mr. Khanna, who set up this place, migrated to the US a few years back. There's a lot to be done, and only me."

I took a DTC bus from the nearest stop, which was another ten-minute walk from Firoza's one-room office in Shahdara. The bus ride all the way to my neighbourhood was a further forty-five minutes. From there, ten minutes to the *basti*, to the house where Tinkle stayed with the woman who looked after her. Almost an hour, and I was on my own, with my thoughts to surround me.

At one moment, it seemed best to turn around and go back. Go to office or go home. Forget about Tinkle. The next moment, that made me feel like the proverbial ostrich, burying its head as deep as it would go into the sand. Pay no attention, and Tinkle would eventually stop leaving those notes in our gate or stuck into the grill of our window.

Eventually, I went all the way to the house. Hut, I should say, because that was what it was: a four walled shack made of mud bricks, two of its walls shared with neighbours. A corrugated tin roof weighed down by heavy stones sat atop the walls. A sagging clothesline ran from the nearby electricity pole to a knot around one of the stones; on it hung an array of faded and misshapen clothes, including a school uniform.

Her name was Kamla. Lotus. She was wiry and strong, the muscles in her forearms working as she squeezed out clothes she had carried back, newly-washed, from somewhere round the corner. I could hear the distinctive kaen-chak-kaen-chak rhythm of a hand pump being worked, the whoosh of water being regurgitated from below the ground up into a bucket.

"She's no relative of mine," Kamla said when I told her what I had come for, and she had satisfied herself that I was above board, innocuous. "Her parents used to live here." She tilted her head, indicating her hut.

"Oh? And?"

"Her father killed someone. Six years ago? I don't remember—it's been a long time. Maybe seven."

She had been draping each wet garment, after she had squeezed it, onto her shoulder. Her blouse was sopping wet by now, the water trickling down to meet the waist of her *sari* where it was tucked into her petticoat. One hand holding the clothes in place, she bent and picked up the last piece of clothing, a ragged green panty. One-handedly, she squeezed it and tucked it in among the rest of the clothes.

"Hmm. Anyway. He was a bad character, that one." She had begun pulling off the dry clothes from the clothesline and now dumped them over the frame of a *charpai* that lay on its side outside the hut. "Went to jail for it, and while he was gone, his wife ran away with someone. I was passing by, and I saw this baby standing out here and crying. Couldn't leave her like that, and nobody around seemed to be bothered." She began hanging up the wet laundry. She'd done a good job of wringing it out; I was impressed.

The long and the short of it was that Kamla had moved into the hut—she didn't say it, but I suspected she might have been homeless to start with. Perhaps a pavement dweller, one of the hundreds who make their homes below Delhi's flyovers. When I asked her about her own family, her own home, she shrugged and said in a bitter sort of way, "Who has family in this city, *didi*?" But she did not answer the question.

It was as I was leaving that she said something that gave me a clue to the truth. "Khanna Sahib was a good man," she said, absent-mindedly, as she gathered up the dry clothes and pulled down the *charpai*, letting its legs come down with a loud bang on the hard ground. "He was a school teacher, you know, before he set up that NGO. He used to come to this *basti* to teach the children. He saw Tinkle when she was four, and he gave me money to send her to school."

A philanthropist, then, I thought. Not many schoolteachers would be so generous, not given what I knew of teachers' salaries. And a teacher who used to teach in a *basti*? Either the man had inherited wealth, or he also tutored the pampered children of wealthy parents who could afford to give their offspring an extra leg up in life.

With her very next words—uttered in a voice so soft I thought I must surely have misheard her—Kamla shattered that illusion. "Tinkle looks exactly like him."

"What?" My voice was a harsh croak.

"Her mother was a slut," she sniggered. "She and her husband, they should never have met, never have married. Although now I wonder if they were even married..." She was folding a *sari* now, its length flapping about in a light breeze that had arisen. "They were the sort of people who live only in the moment. Selfish, completely selfish. They could not really ever love anybody but themselves. The child was an accident. An unwanted accident."

"How do you know all this?" I whispered. "If you weren't even here—"

"Everybody in the *basti* knows it," she said. "Ask anyone. There are people who will even tell you how Khanna Sahib used to come to visit her every day on his way back from the teaching the *basti* children. *Every day*. While her husband was out. Nobody guessed when the baby was born, but by the time she was a few months old, it became apparent. She looked too much like Khanna Sahib to be anybody but his."

That, as Kamla told it, was the reason Mr Khanna had given her money to bring up Tinkle. To teach her, most importantly. "But he went away," she said as she gathered up her pile of neatly folded clothes. "For a few years, he still sent me money. Now even that has stopped. I've got no money for the past two months."

"Have you written to him to ask? Maybe it's stuck somewhere—"

She interrupted me with a harsh laugh. "Me? Do you think I can write? Do you think I even know where he lives? He could be on the moon for all I know." She gave me an odd look. "Go away, *didi*. Go away, go back to your own life. We will live our lives as we can."

As I walked slowly back home, I wondered what she had meant. Would she somehow find the means to keep Tinkle in school? Or if not in school, at least clothed and fed? How, if, as I suspected, Kamla herself had been a pavement dweller before she took over as Tinkle's foster mother? Or caregiver, or whatever one wanted to label her. It was informal; it was probably not even something Kamla wanted to do. Never once in our conversation had I heard her refer to Tinkle by name, even. Somehow I could not see her going out of her way to bother about the child. Tinkle would, most likely, be abandoned all over again.

And there she was, sitting on that broken-off stump of concrete, her head bent over her notebook, scribbling. I stopped; she was far enough away for me to not be able to see her features, close enough for me to recognize her as Tinkle. I could have walked on, pretended to be a passerby. I could have waited until she had written her note and left it in its customary place. I did not need to involve myself in this child's life.

But I had. By going to her school, by meeting Firoza, by talking to Kamla. None of them would expect me to do anything about it, I guessed, but I could not pretend nothing had shifted in my life. If nothing else, I had to—at least once—talk to this girl.

"Are you writing to your mother?" I asked. She was so startled, she jumped up, struggling to stuff her notebook into the shabby schoolbag that had been in her lap, acting as a makeshift desk. She didn't say anything; she just looked terrified. I tried to give her a soothing smile.

"I live in that house," I said, indicating our home. 'Would you like to come in? For a glass of juice?"

As soon as I had said it, I regretted it. She shook her head vigorously. God alone knows what kept her still glued to the place; she looked as if she would bolt any moment.

"Can I sit here, then?" I asked, my voice soft. "I would like to, if you don't mind. Is that your bottle? Can I have some water?" I had noticed a recycled Pepsi one litre bottle standing in the grass beside the concrete block. "I'm very thirsty," I added. And it was true: my throat was parched. The last time I had drunk water had been in the principal's office. Firoza had offered me water too, but I had refused, since I had thought then that I would soon be in my own office anyway. And Kamla had not even offered me a place to sit, let alone a glass of water.

Tinkle looked a little taken aback, but it seemed to break the spell. She picked up the bottle and held it out. Thoughts raced through my mind, one following the other. I could have chosen some other way to befriend her. I could have waited a few more minutes and drunk water when I was back home. This water was surely full of stuff I didn't want to know about. Where had it come from? The hand pump I had heard near Kamla's hut?

It was lukewarm, but it tasted like any other water. Like the water at home, the water at my office. I had meant to take only a tentative sip, no more. I ended up gulping down much more. When I put the bottle down, there was only a swallow left in it. I felt guilty. This little girl had shared what was surely a precious commodity for her, and I had greedily finished off much more than she had expected. "I'm sorry," I said. 'I've drunk up more than I had meant to."

She shook her head. "My home is not far. I don't need more."

"You are Tinkle, aren't you?" I asked. "I … I read your letters. I didn't know they were meant for your mother."

She stared at me. A pretty little girl, her skin the colour of milky *chai*, with a patina of deep gold tan. Large expressive eyes, a small mouth. Thin arms and legs, bony ankles around which socks that had lost their elastic a long time back had settled. The school uniform, as I had guessed when I had first seen her from afar, was something made to last as long as it possibly could: something she would literally grow into. She was still too small for it. It was already faded, the collar frayed and the shirt a dirty white that would never be pristine, no matter how much it was washed in the water from that hand pump.

"Why did you put the letters there?" I asked, my voice as gentle as I could make it. "In our gate? In the window grill?"

She shook her head, as if trying to deny she had done it. Then, perhaps realizing that it was no use, she mumbled, "I won't do it again. I ... I'm sorry."

"There's nothing to be sorry about." I moved a little on the concrete block so that I was sitting half off the edge, and patted the little space that had been cleared. "Come and sit down. Tell me about your mother."

She did not know anything about her mother, of course. Kamla had made it clear that she wasn't Tinkle's mother, but she had said nothing of who was her mother. "I don't know what she looks like, even," Tinkle said, her voice so low that I had to strain to hear it. "Kamla *didi* says it is better I don't know. How can that be? How is it good for me to not know my own mother?"

Tears had welled up in her eyes, tears, I could tell, of loneliness and frustration. I could imagine what people must tell this child when she asked about her mother. Not just Kamla, but everybody else around. *Forget her, she's gone, she won't be back.* They would be seeing it from the point of view of society, a society that took pride in its righteous indignation at the bad ways of a woman who had run away with another man, leaving her child behind. Who knew why Tinkle's mother had run away? Perhaps her husband beat her; perhaps life had become unbearable for her in his house. Perhaps the man she had run off with was just a means of getting her to a better place, a place where she could be safe, secure.

I could understand that. Just as easily as I could understand that Tinkle wanted her mother. It would not matter to this child if her mother were a slut, a whore, worthy of all the foul epithets society heaped on her. The mother could be all of that, and still a mother.

Without even thinking about it, I put my arm around her shoulders. I did not pull her to me, even though she was sobbing now. I did not tell her to hush. I know what it is like. I have wept a lot.

Ours is a quiet little lane; most people travelling between the main road and the *basti* prefer to take the wider road, which runs parallel to this, because that's where the buses stop, that's where the autos are to be found. Even then, even with the very meagre traffic, there were those who turned to look at us. At a woman and a girl sitting on a shared block of discarded concrete. Weeping, both woman and girl. Alone, yet together.

Perhaps someday we will both be able to find those we miss. Tinkle's mother will come back, loving and maternal, her arms open and her heart full of love. Perhaps that unseen Mr Khanna—if he really is Tinkle's father and not a poor benevolent soul who merely happened to frequent their house—will return. If he is not dead.

Someday, too, perhaps my son will be given to me. Perhaps the court will grant me custody of Abhay. Or if that does not happen, perhaps someday, when he realizes how much his mother loves him, he will come looking for me.

Until then, we will go on missing these people. My son, her mother. We will sit together and listen to each other echoing what we think. We will imagine ourselves in the other's place.

"A girl from school told me that there was a woman in this house who looked like me," Tinkle says, looking up shyly at me. Her cheeks are still damp, but she is not crying any more. "I thought it might be my mother."

"Me?" I smile. "Yes, we do look a little alike, don't we?"

She smiles back. No, it is not a mirror of my own smile, but at least we are both smiling. And the smiles are genuine. I can see it in her eyes. And I am mirrored in her eyes.

Mushrooms and Memory

MONICA MENEGHETTI

M Y ITALIAN MOTHER adored mushrooms. You mustn't imagine white, supermarket mushrooms. Instead, imagine moss-adorned mushrooms hugged by decaying leaves. Mushrooms whose caps know the shiatsu of rain and understand the responsibility of umbrellas. The kind that turn as black as squid ink and slide like oil against your tongue when sautéed.

Imagine wild mushrooms: puffballs, porcini, and russula. Foraged personally. Eased by hand out of the soil from the very base of their stems so as not to tear away any identifying parts. Mushrooms birthed by earth and still dangling mycelial threads.

My mom loved foraging for mushrooms. She called it *andare a funghi. Andare a funghi* means "to go mushrooming." But I prefer the literal translation "to go to mushrooms." It evokes a pilgrimage, a quest for a grail, a whiff of the mountain going to Mohammad.

Mushrooms cannot make their own food. They take nutrients from the roots of green plants, from dead organic matter, from feces and soil.

In the same way, memory cannot create experience. It depends on human life, on the life of the human brain. Memory sustains itself on metabolites of perception—what we call "the past"—on the excreta of consciousness and the humus of layer upon layer of moments.

I don't remember much of my life before the age of ten. My mom died when I was sixteen. My connection to her depends on a mere six-year span of memory. And when I delve into that precious pond of images and impressions, I often encounter gaps.

I remember how much she loved going to mushrooms. But what did she wear? How did she move? I only know there was a hat of some sort. And a basket.

My earliest memory of going to mushrooms: my father putting what seemed like a bushel of mushrooms into the trunk of our baby blue Plymouth Belvedere. He hid them under a Bolivian blanket, ignoring my mom's protests as he drove out of the parking lot.

Fines for mushrooming in a Banff national park can go into the thousands of dollars. But I didn't know about fines back then. I only knew my dad was trying to get away with something. Mom hated this as much as I did. The feeling it gave me was familiar from airport customs checks.

We'd come back from Italy once with suitcases full of expensive goods. He didn't declare most of it. A queen-sized camel hair blanket. A dozen or more shirts made of *filo di seta*, shiny silk thread. When I remember Dad in those days, he's always wearing one of these shirts in saffron yellow or navy blue. They were form fitting with pointy, boned collars and a breast pocket over the heart into which he sometimes put his Polaroid aviators.

I don't recall any sweat stains on his silk shirt as he glided past customs pushing that loaded luggage cart. Meanwhile, my scalp prickled and my belly felt full and empty at the same time. I gripped my mom's hand and avoided eye contact with big uniformed men, other travellers, cleaning staff—anyone, really. My fear was not as much of him getting caught as it was of being the one to give him away. I was incapable of telling a convincing lie.

I felt that same fear as we drove east and approached the national park gates with a trunk full of fungal contraband. But there was no check point, no uniformed guard. After a few kilometres, Mom and I stopped checking behind us for red-and-blue flashing lights.

Was that clandestine foraging the genesis of my parents' mushroom plan? As my mom stooped to pick a choice edible that day, was my dad transfixed by her singular joy? Perhaps love led him to give his wife a gift: eighty acres of land where she could go to the mushrooms without fear of fines.

I like to imagine them waking up together on a Sunday morning. My mother reaching out for her husband before her eyes even open and whispering, "*Andiamo a funghi.*"

As fungi feed on plant nutrients, they release enzymes, thus producing essential elements for plants. They release antibiotics, offering protection from bacterial infection. Fungi loosen soil, easing movement of air and water.

Memory feeds experience, transforming quotidian acts into soul-sustaining moments. Memory strikes life like a bell so that we may bathe in resonance. Memory inoculates us against oblivion. In the moment of recall, memory slackens our control, freeing the heart to join the blood in its visitation of every cell.

To get to the mushrooms, we had to drive for a few hours. This meant we had to endure the surging and lagging sensations caused by Dad's inconsistent pressure on the gas pedal. It meant fumigating in a sealed chamber of Rothmans King-sized smoke. It wasn't as much a drive as a melty, stretchy, rewinding clock's worth of Dali-esque nausea and asphyxia.

Once we arrived at our property, Dad would lift a loop of barbed wire over a wooden post to pull the fence open. He'd line the car tires up with ruts in the ground and park just inside the fence. I would have my door open before he even cut the engine, eager to dive into the fresh air and silence. It was like snorkelling in tranquillity.

Then, Dad popped the trunk. Accompanied by the ping of a cooling engine, we slung little canvas *zainini* onto our backs. Mom would don her denim bucket hat and take her square rattan basket in hand.

We would leave the car behind, tall grass bent beneath the chassis. The brush of the same grass against our jeans created a static of peace, the soundtrack for the start of a beautiful day.

We'd begin to scan the ground immediately, like pigs hunting truffles. A network of footpaths and animal trails took us into thick bush. Following our instincts toward the mushrooms, we'd sometimes find ourselves foraging alone, out of sight of one another.

I was never afraid of getting lost. I told myself, "Keep walking until you hit the fence and follow that fence to a corner and then another until you find the car." Besides, we had blazed a trail toward our meeting place. I simply followed orange surveyor tape or hatchet-marked tree trunks to reach the clearing we dubbed Cathedral Square.

Cathedral Square wasn't just any old *piazza* with a crumbling church. It was a square we'd cleared ourselves. In it, we stood on humus, not masonry. We had branches instead of flying buttresses and sky for a cupola. Our fire pit within a tripod of saplings inspired more reverence than any altar, past or present.

The journey to Cathedral Square. Now *that* was the important part of the day. Without it, the square was only a picnic area and the fire just a grill for hotdogs.

I would wander in the trees, sensing everything. Solitary but not alone. Mom and Dad were out there somewhere. I could yodel out to them anytime. The silence flowed around me as intimately as warm water.

Once, in that stillness, Mom's voice reached me. The vibration of her sound resounded from wood and air and dappled light. It was an amalgam of song, yodel, and exclamation. It was her joy-cry, set free as she found a rare choice edible at the foot of an evergreen.

In that moment, through her voice, my mom had beamed herself to me; suddenly, she was with me. I didn't know exactly where she was. But I knew—more than ever before or since—I knew *that* she was.

This is my only memory of the sound of her voice. Sometimes, when I spot a mushroom's soft crown emerging from the earth, I can hear her calling out to me.

Monica Meneghetti's "Mushrooms and Memory" is an excerpt of the piece previously published in her memoir, What the Mouth Wants: A Memoir of Food, Love and Belonging *(Dagger Editions, 2017).*

The Orchard

MONICA MENEGHETTI

I AWAKE FEELING AS IF someone is calling me. Dad's snoring usually travels through doors and walls to every room of the house, but the house is quiet. I hear my clock ticking and turn in bed to read its glowing hands: two o'clock in the morning. I reach for my shawl and run my fingertips over the stitches, remembering how every millimetre of yarn ran through Mom's hands as she knit it for me. I wrap it around my shoulders, push my feet into sheepskin slippers then open the door. Down the hallway, my parents' bedside lamp glows. I walk toward the light.

Mom lies in the big bed, as she has since the day of my brother's wedding a month before. The blankets dip slightly on the side where her left breast once was. Her jaw is settled back slightly, making it seem she has an overbite, and her high cheek bones stand out as in her leaner youth. Her thin hair, carefully combed, looks accidental against the pillow. Her big, green eyes are open but immobile. Has it been only days since she's stopped tracking our movements? The nurse from the Victorian Order told us to expect this. As Mom gets nearer to death, she will appear to be asleep, but we won't be able to wake her because she'll be in a coma.

I look across at Dad, who is sitting next to Mom on the bed. His close-set eyes seem closer together than ever. He's slept little for the last month, fearful of leaving Mom in pain by missing even one dose of painkillers. I know that hearing her in distress, he wakes to comfort her. He's told me she's been asking why it is taking so long to die. There are layoffs in the oil patch, too, so he goes to work each day taut with the dread of losing his job. I pried into the Victorian Order of Nurses file the last time they were here, so I know they are watching out for him. They noted the number of espressos he has been drinking, among other concerns.

My parents' arguments still blaze vivid in my memory. Not long ago, I wondered if they were only staying together because of me, the last kid left at home. That made me feel guilty, and I resolved to grow up as quickly as possible. Now as I watch Dad caress Mom's cheek and whisper something to her in Italian, I wonder if I understand what love really means.

I haven't slept much myself. The other day, I fell asleep at school in front of my locker with my ear crushed against my Modern Biology textbook. I feel guilty about that, too. Unlike my Dad, I'm not losing sleep nursing Mom. Instead, I'm writing the last part of my story, *Indian Summer: The Season to Fall*. I glance again at Mom. Her fixed gaze brings the first lines of my story to mind: *Miranda was half Cherokee and half blind. Her lifetime was more than half over.*

My Mom's sister is sitting beside the bed. Her mood is hard to read, so I opt for kissing her on the cheek rather than saying anything.

"*Ciao, tesoro,*" my aunt says softly.

Dad encourages her to go to bed. True, it is late, and my *Zia* has been there for hours despite jet-lag from her trans-Atlantic flight, but I sense an undercurrent of unease.

I know my Mom's sister is exquisitely sensitive. Maybe their childhood had something to do with it.

She and Mom were raised in a convent in the foothills of the Italian Alps. Their mother, a travelling saleswoman raising them alone, felt her daughters would be safer there from the war. Although they escaped the worst of the air raids, the convent left other scars. Mom told me about kneeling on the stone floor of the cathedral until she fainted from pain and exhaustion. The nuns tied her left hand behind her back, insisting she become right handed because the left hand was *sinistra*, the evil hand. If the children stained their hands or clothes when dipping nibs into inkwells, the nuns would make them dip their fingers into human feces as punishment. Parents would bring scarce items like powdered milk to the convent and the nuns would feast on it, while the children roamed the woods looking for berries and mushrooms to fill their empty bellies. Once, while scavenging, a girl fell into an uncapped, abandoned outhouse hole and nearly drowned in rotting excrement. Mom had railed at the injustice, incurring more severe punishment than the other children. Through it all, she protected her sister from the worst of the blows and held it together, the practical one who shielded her more vulnerable older sister.

Little wonder that Mom never mentioned God or went to church, and I am almost an atheist despite years of Catholic school. But still, she wanted the final sacrament. A priest performed Extreme Unction last week, and the change in her was incredible. After weeks of feeling agitated and afraid, she became profoundly peaceful. What will do that for me, I wonder, when it's my time?

"*Dai*," Dad says to *Zia*, reassuring her that it is okay to go to bed. She relents, finally admitting fatigue.

"Wake me up as soon as something starts happening." She wants us to promise before she will leave, so we do, and she kisses her sister so gently that lips and cheek barely touch.

I take the chair beside the bed, put a pillow on my lap, and settle in with my best friend's graphic novel, *Ronin*. I flip through it, scanning superbly drawn images of bloody battles and murder. I stare at the page while my mind wanders back to my story.

Miranda lives on her orchard with an acquaintance named Seth, who is impatiently awaiting her death. They both have no one, so she knows that he offers kindness only out of hope of inheriting her orchard. One day, she says her time is complete and asks Seth to help her end it...

I adjust the pillow in my lap and glance up at Mom. I should have been with her, or helping Dad instead of writing that story. But Mom knows I dreamed of being a writer. Ever since I wrote my first story on a manual Olivetti in grade five, she'd known it. She always bought me books featuring characters who were writers, like *Little House on the Prairie*, and *Are You There God? It's Me, Margaret*. And she brought me notebooks, *quaderni*, whenever she came home from Italy. I am used to grade school exercise books, manila covers bearing the Calgary Catholic School District logo in black ink. But those glossy, patterned and colourful *quaderni* seem to come from another planet entirely. Whether the pages are lined or unlined or graph paper, I fill up every one, feeling my dreams are bound to come true. That very year, she argued with overprotective Dad to allow me take my first writing workshop. And it turned out to be worth it. I finally wrote a good story. Mom would be happy for me, wouldn't she?

Over the past months, I began taking care of Mom. At first, she was outright mean to me. Maybe she was trying to protect me by pushing me away. But Mom is very proud and independent, so I figure she just wanted to do things for herself. Like Miranda did.

... Miranda had enjoyed Seth at first. She was wise to his manoeuvres and often had to keep herself from laughing. And she loved to frustrate him by hanging on to her life for one more week, and then another and still another. But it was getting harder to enjoy Seth, with his smells of gasoline, beer, and wet socks. As she lost the energy to work in the orchard, he was useful but no longer amusing. As the weeks went by, Miranda asked more and more of him. The thought of being dependent on a man like Seth made Miranda feel weak. It made her feel old....

Eventually, Mom stopped resisting my presence. Dad wasn't sure at first whether it was wise to let me help, but wound up relenting, probably out of exhaustion. He made a point of doing the harder work himself, though, like helping her to the bathroom and later, onto the bedpan.

After school, while my friends hung out in the tire park, smoking while strategizing about how to get alcohol and lose their virginity, I took care of my forty-nine-year-old Mom. I'd bring her *minestra*, spoon soup into her mouth, and wipe her chin. Later, I'd make her a cup of *camomilla* and smooth *crema Nivea* on her chapped lips. Whenever one of us didn't feel well, she would always say, "*Metti cremina!*" or steep some tea for us. Nivea and chamomile are Mom's panaceas, and I used them on her, hoping they would work.

Now, as I sit beside the bed, I wonder if Mom is glad to have me with her. I look up from the graphic novel, search her face for some expression. "*Guarda con gli occhi della mente,*" Mom admonishes when I can't find something in the cupboards. Look with your mind's eye. But I still can't tell whether she even knows I am there.

Before long, her breathing gets very loud. I listen as if to a strange music. Each breath is a beat, and the pause between beats lengthens. Each breath comes with more effort, as though she needs every ounce of strength to complete this simple thing she's done unconsciously all of her life. It sounds like something is loose inside her chest. I imagine ribs suspended from strings, chiming together as the air rushes past them.

Dad whispers to Mom, then looks at me and says, "She's going." I put my fingers on her wrist, search for and find a weak pulse. The pause between breaths becomes so long that we think each is her last, but then another heaves through the silence, and we watch her face, and wait.

Finally, no other breaths come, and I feel the pulse in her wrist grow fainter. I feel it stop.

"I can't find a pulse," I tell Dad. I check again. Nothing.

I remember our promise to *Zia*. "I should go get her," I say, but Dad wants to clean her up a little first, make the sight less shocking for her. So I wait. Too late now anyway.

Dad wipes Mom's mouth. Then draws her eyelids shut. One of them won't close. The day before, I wrote ... *It was done. Seth stepped jauntily toward the half-ton truck. Its one remaining headlight stared at him so steadily, it could well have been Miranda's eye, the one that didn't close. It stared right at him, accusing him. Seth didn't care....*

I sit motionless and emotionless. The seemingly prophetic nature of my words and an uncanny combination of facts combine to form a strange chant: One eye open. Three in the morning. Father's Day. I was born at 3 a.m.

Dad pulls aside the covers. I can't remember the last time I saw my mother in her underwear. Not long ago, she yanked down my blinds when she found me changing in front of the unshielded window. I still hear her admonishing me, *"Abbia un pò di pudore!"*—have some modesty. And now here I am, watching as Dad cleans and changes Mom into a fresh nightgown. I look away. One eye open. Three in the morning. Father's Day. Born at 3 a.m. "It's pretty simple, really, this death thing," I say to Dad. It seems real when people die on TV. But now I know it isn't, it isn't like on TV at all. Not full of action, not even a dramatic moment like in my story.

Now I know the truth about death. A very quiet moment, very natural, so subtle you can miss it. One second a heart is beating and the next it isn't. Between one pulse and another, a whole life is over. Everything you learned, everything you remember, all gone. Just like that. And I know the same will be true for me. I vow to live enough life for the both of us.

Once Dad is satisfied with how Mom looks, I go to my brother's old room, where *Zia* is sleeping. She's flown across the ocean to sit at her sister's deathbed, wanting to be there with her at the end. Now she's lost that too. I say her name before softly touching her shoulder but she still jumps. I search for words, borrow my Dad's "She's gone." *Zia* gets up in a flurry of blankets, swings on her robe, then rushes at me, hitting me feebly with her fists, shouting, "I told you to come get me, I told you!" I hold her up in my arms for a moment, feeling nothing. I follow her as she rushes down the hall.

Zia croons her sister's name through sobs. She begins smoothing the body's hair, caressing the cheek.

How weird. It's as if she believes she's talking to Mom, but Mom's not in there. Maybe that's what *Zia's* eyes know, why they are darting here and there on the landscape of Mom's face, over and over, searching for signs of her.

Dad asks me to call the funeral home. They have all the information, so I only have to notify them. I go downstairs to the kitchen and find the number on the cork board.

Next to the phone, among other odds and ends, is the beautiful cloisonné box I bought for Mom. I meant it for her chemo pills. She flatly refused to use it. "They are pills, not candies," she said.

I fiddle with the box and listen to the dial tone while staring at the countertop. Suddenly, I see its white surface arrayed with our last haul of wild mushrooms, hear Mom's hoots of joy coming from somewhere through the trees as she discovers first one, then another choice edible for wild mushroom *risotto* or *funghi trifolati*.

Finally, I dial the number.

"You've reached McInnis and Holloway. How can I help you?"

"Yes, um, hello. Um ... my mom is dead now."

"I'm sorry for your loss. Who's calling?"

"Meneghetti."

Next thing I know, a doctor arrives. He puts a stethoscope to the body's chest in several places, listening as though there is a chance he'll hear something. I laugh. I have already felt the silence he is hearing. His actions are a charade. He fills out paperwork certifying she is dead. "I could have told you that," I say. What's that look he gives me? Pity?

Then a procession of people come; it seems endless. All of them touching and talking to the body. I dismiss them as fools. Two men arrive carrying a black board and a purple blanket. Everyone else leaves, but I am curious to see everything. They lift Mom's corpse—for that's what it is now, isn't it?—onto the board. Once they arrange the blanket over her body, I rub the fabric between my thumb and forefinger. The inside of the blanket is cool and satiny. The outside is a warm velvet. Why would they put the velvety side out instead of in, against her skin? Oh. Because Mom is dead. The blanket isn't meant to soothe *her*. It's meant for us.

I follow the undertakers out the front door. The hearse is parked beneath our big poplar tree. How can the leaves look yellow when I smell the fresh fragrance of bright June green? What's wrong with me?

When the men open the back doors, the grey satin valences on the back windows swing slightly. Once they slide the board onto the grey-carpeted interior, I turn and walk back up the driveway and into the kitchen.

I see Mom sweeping the kitchen floor in her housedress, as she has every day for as long as I can remember. An Italian cassette is playing, the one that *Zia* sent, and Mom is singing along.

After this life that forgets you,
After this sky without a rainbow
After this melancholy, these lies
After all this longing for peace
Tell me, who will there be?

Suddenly, she inhales sharply, bracing herself against the table. The cancer has spread to her liver and any bending motion causes terrible pain. I try to take the broom from her, but she yanks it back. We both stand alone, crying.

There will be
A shadow at your side, dressed in white

There will be
A kinder way to say, "I love you."
My sister's voice pulls me away from my memory.

"I guess this is our job now," she says, unloading the dishwasher.

"Actually, it's been our job for a while already," I say, opening the cutlery drawer and taking a handful of spoons from her. Their shiny curves nestle together in the tray. I find it comforting.

* * *

I bend over and shake my hair, tossing it back as I straighten. Got to look good. If my name is called for the Grade 11 English Award, I will be up on stage in front of the whole school. I turn sideways and look at my belly in the mirror. Good. It's not sticking out very far today. I hear the garburator-like sound of the garage door lifting, my cue that Dad's ready to leave. I take one last look in the mirror and rush down the stairs and out to the car.

The passenger seat is empty. Otherwise, everything's the same. My sister sitting beside me in the back seat. Dad chain smoking Rothmans with the windows sealed shut so the air conditioning works. The slipped disc in his back causing an uneven pressure on the gas pedal so that the car lurches forward and lags back, forward and back, making me feel carsick, as usual.

The linoleum floors of my high school shine with new polish. Dad, my sister, and I walk past the award cases lining the entrance hall. I've seen them day after day for the past two years, but now the cases seem larger, fuller. Will my name be engraved on one of the trophies for all to see, now and in coming years? My stomach flutters. But Dad and my sister don't seem excited. Of course not. Mom died just a few days ago. What kind of daughter could care about an award at a time like this? But I do.

Being at school after supper is strange. The deserted halls seem longer, narrower. Unopened lockers line the walls like tiles and their silver locks are like the identical links of a chain.

It's a relief to get to the gym, which is alive with students, teachers, and parents. The sliding panels on the far wall of the gym are open to the stage. Drama students are checking the stage lights, and the heavy velvet curtains are pulled aside to reveal the black floor and scrim. Chairs are set up in rows, leaving a runway down the centre for the award winners to approach the stage.

My sister and I both look up at the stage. "I feel pretteeee, oh so pretteeee," she sings half-heartedly. I bat my lashes, clasp my hands together beside my cheek, and reply, "I feel prettee and witteee and briiiight, and I piteee any girl who isn't meeee tooonight!" We chuckle a bit, remembering the Westside Story production she danced in on this stage a few years ago.

I spot one of the popular kids. Her sleek, blonde hair is perfect, and her corduroys must be a size one. If only I win the award! That'll show her. I fiddle with my belt, making sure my shirt's tucked in flat over my belly.

Mr. Bedard, the teacher who made me work hard on my stories for the first time, smiles at me from across the gym. My English teacher, Mr. MacIlhone, waves at me from the stage. A good sign? My stomach flutters again. No, they're probably just being extra nice because of what happened.

Dad finds some seats, and we settle into them. I try to pay attention while the other awards are presented so I can clap at the right times. Then, finally, the English awards start. I'm excited, but Dad's distracted, looking down at his palms. I think he might fall asleep. My sister's in her own world, too. I fix my hair and wonder why I'm not sad, like them. I should be, shouldn't I? Is there something wrong with me?

"I was blessed with a gifted group of young people this year," says Mr. MacIlhone. "And one of those students has earned this year's English Award." So! It's going to be someone from my class! Maybe that cutie who loves the Doors and writes those sci-fi stories?

"Congratulations to … Monica Meneghetti! Come on up here and get your trophy."

In a daze, I slide out to the aisle and start walking toward the stage. The gym floor is waxy, and my shoes stick to it a little. Looking down at my feet, I see fragmented lines in red, black, green, blue, and it takes me a moment to realize they are basketball court lines, criss-crossing the aisle. I jog up the stairs to the stage, hoping my boobs don't bounce too much. And then I'm beside Mr. MacIlhone hoping I don't look fat, and he's waiting for me to shake his hand. Beside him is Mr. Bedard, holding a huge trophy that gleams white and gold. Handing it to me he says, "Your name will be engraved on it later this week," and winks. Somehow, it doesn't feel as great as I imagined. I stand with them both, smile my best smile for the camera. Then they take the trophy away, into the wings.

Back at the seats, no one seems happy for me. Dad is wiping his eyes with a tissue. My sister tidies her mascara with an index finger. I stare at the bouquet of white roses in my arms, wondering how they got there. Wondering who will buy me notebooks now.

In the car, I hear a female voice: "*Ti piaciono le rose?*" *Do I like the roses*. The words seem to be coming from where Mom usually sits. Confused, I look up. *Zia* is looking back at me from the passenger seat. Why hadn't I seen her there before? They're from mamma, she tells me. She would be so proud of you.

Dad lurches the car toward home. I'm not sure I like roses.

Monica Meneghetti's "The Orchard" was previously published in her memoir, What the Mouth Wants: A Memoir of Food, Love and Belonging *(Dagger Editions, 2017).*

About the Contributors

Berit Åström, PhD, is an associate professor at the Department of Language Studies at Umeå University, Sweden. Having published on male pregnancy fan fiction and the concept of "referred pain" in Shakespeare, she is currently working on representations of motherhood. Among her recent publications is "The Symbolic Annihilation of Mothers in Popular Culture: *Single Father* and the Death of the Mother," published in *Feminist Media Studies*, 2015.

Courtney Bates-Hardy is a poet and the executive director of the Saskatchewan Book Awards. She is the author of *House of Mystery* (ChiZine Publications, 2016). She holds a Master's degree in creative writing from the University of Regina. Her poems have appeared in a variety of literary magazines, including *Room, Carousel,* and *On Spec.* Her poems have been featured in *Imaginarium 4: The Best Canadian Speculative Writing* and longlisted for *The Best Canadian Poetry 2015.* She lives in Regina with her husband and their cat, Jean Grey.

Bianca Batti is a PhD student in literary studies in the English department at Purdue University, where she studies twentieth- and twenty-first century American literature. She received her MA in English at San Diego State University and her BA in literature and writing at the University of California at San Diego. Her current research engages in feminist analyses of representations of motherhood and gendered labour in contemporary American literature.

Corinna Chong is a writer, editor, and graphic designer based in Kelowna, BC. Her first novel, *Belinda's Rings*, was published by NeWest Press in 2013. Her short story, "Porcelain Legs" appears in *AlliterAsian: Twenty Years of Ricepaper Magazine*, an anthology (Arsenal Pulp Press). She has also published stories and reviews in *Room Magazine, Malahat Review, Grain,* and others.

Emma Dalton is an Independent Researcher. She recently completed her PhD in the Theatre and Drama Program at La Trobe University in Melbourne, Australia. She has a Bachelor of Performing Arts (Honours) from Monash University and a Master of Arts from La Trobe University. Dalton has two prior publications, "Maternal Practice and Maternal Presence in Jane Harrison's Stolen" (published by *Outskirts Online Journal* in 2015) and "Maternal Resilience and Preservative Love in Joanna Murray-Smith's Pennsylvania Avenue" (published as part of *The Australasian Association for Theatre, Drama, and Performance Studies 2016 Conference Proceedings*). Dalton's PhD thesis investigates the representation of mothers in contemporary Australian female-authored play-texts and live performances.

Frances Greenslade has a BA in English from the University of Winnipeg and an MFA in creative writing from University of British Columbia. *By the Secret Ladder* and *A Pilgrim in Ireland* (Penguin) are her first two books, both memoirs. Her novel, *Shelter*, was published in Canada by Random House in 2011, in the U.S. by Free Press and the UK by Virago in 2012. It has been translated into Dutch, German, and Italian. She has taught English and creative writing at Okanagan College since 2005.

Sarah de Leeuw, PhD, is an associate professor in the Northern Medical Program at UNBC. An award-winning researcher and creative writer whose work focuses broadly on marginalized peoples and geographies, de Leeuw grew up and has spent most of her life in Northern British Columbia, including Haida Gwaii and Terrace. She is the research director of the Health Arts Research Centre and teaches in the areas of Indigenous peoples' wellbeing and health humanities. Her books include *Determinants*

116

of *Indigenous Peoples' Health in Canada: Beyond the Social* (Canadian Scholars' Press, 2015) and *Skeena,* a book of poetry published by Caitlin Press.

Madhulika Liddle is a novelist and award-winning short story writer. Though popularly known as the author of the Muzaffar Jang series, featuring a seventeenth-century Mughal detective, Liddle also writes short stories in various genres. Her story, *A Morning Swim,* won the Overall Prize in the Commonwealth Broadcasting Association's Short Story Competition in 2003. In 2016, she became the first Indian to be longlisted for the prestigious Sunday Times EFG Short Story Award for her story *Poppies in the Snow.* In addition, Liddle blogs about classic cinema, travel, food and history, at www.madhulikaliddle.com.

Randy Lundy is a member of the Barren Lands (Cree) First Nation, Brochet, MB, but he has lived most of his life in Saskatchewan. He completed a BA (honours) and an MA in English at the University of Saskatchewan. He has two books of poetry, *Under the Night Sun* and *Gift of the Hawk. Blackbird Song* will be published in 2017. His poetry has been widely anthologized, including in the seminal texts *Native Poetry in Canada: A Contemporary Anthology* and *An Anthology of Canadian Native Literature in English.* His poetry has appeared in anthologies in the United States, New Zealand, and Australia. Lundy teaches Indigenous literatures and creative writing in the English Department at Campion College, University of Regina.

Monica Meneghetti's poetry and fiction have been published in *The Winnipeg Review, Prairie Journal, Prairie Fire, Filling Station* and *Canadian Alpine Journal,* while her creative nonfiction is found online with *CBC Canada Writes, CBC Hyperlocal, Trivia: Voices of Feminism* and *Plenitude Magazine.* Her lyrics feature in the scores of Canadian composers Luciane Cardassi, Nova Pon, and Diana McIntosh. Her first work of literary translation, *The Call of the Ice* (Mountaineer's Books, 2014), was a finalist in the 2015 Banff Mountain Book Competition. Monica released her memoir, *What the Mouth Wants: A Memoir of Food, Love* *and Belonging* (Dagger Editions, 2017), this spring. She's proud to be a part of the forthcoming anthology supporting refugee and low-income families, *Sustenance: Writers from B.C. and Beyond on the Subject of Food* (Anvil Press) edited by Vancouver's Poet Laureate Rachel Rose. She lives on unceded territory of the Musqueam, Squamish and Tsleil-Waututh First Nations (Vancouver, Canada).

Subimal Misra has been called the only anti-establishment writer in Bengali. Influenced by the cinema of Sergei Eisenstein and Jean-Luc Godard, Misra experimented with the use of film language in Bengali writing. With his very first collection of stories, *Haran Majhi's Widow's Corpse or the Golden Gandhi Statue* (1971), he signalled his departure from conventional narrative fiction. He has written exclusively for little magazines. Misra's stories, novelettes, novellas, novels, essays, and interviews comprise over thirty volumes. *Cupid's Corpse Does Not Drown in Water*, an experimental prose-work, was published in 2010. He lives in Kolkata, India.

V. Ramaswamy lives in Kolkata, India. His translations of the short fiction of Subimal Misra include *The Golden Gandhi Statue from America* (2010) and *Wild Animals Prohibited* (2015).

Esther Ramsay-Jones is a PhD student, funded by the Faculty of Social Sciences at the Open University. She is supervised by Gail Lewis at Birkbeck College, University of London, and Dr Peter Redman at the Open University. As part of this work, she had the opportunity to conduct a year-long infant observation of a mum and baby pairing. Before this she worked in the field of dementia care as a frontline worker, and in training and development. She is a practising psychodynamic psychotherapist, counsellor, and a mum. Some of her written and digital video work has been published in publications, such as *Studies in the Maternal* and *Psychodynamic Practice*. Recently she has been working on a poetry blog, which relates to her experiences of being with older people with dementia: https://dailyinfidelities.wordpress.com/tag/dementia.

Bernadette Wagner is a multigenre writer, editor, instructor, and speaker whose collection of poetry, *This hot place* (Thistledown Press, 2010), was shortlisted for the Saskatchewan First Book Award. A recent essay, "A Bad Law and a Bold Woman," appears in the anthology, *Without Apology: Writings on Abortion in Canada* (Athabasca University Press, 2016). Wagner is currently fine tuning a new collection of poetry, revising a manuscript of children's poetry, and adding words to two creative nonfiction manuscripts.